Mineral Resource Governance and Human Development in Ghana

I0123550

This book investigates how mineral resources can be governed to promote people-centred development in Ghana, focusing on the three main human development variables: living standards, education and health.

Ghana is endowed with abundant mineral resources. The mineral sector accounts for about 14% of total tax revenue, driven mostly by an increase in export earnings from the gold sector and the commencement of crude oil exports. However, the country has not yet been able to use its natural resources to promote human development, and the majority of the population still lives on less than $2 a day. This book argues for a paradigm shift in the discussion of mineral resources, one that looks to govern natural resources in such a way as to improve standards of living, health, education, income levels, empowerment, quality of work and threats from violence. The human-centred mineral resource governance approach developed by this book will not only be useful to Ghana, but can also be applied to other mineral-rich countries in sub-Saharan Africa.

This book will be important to upper-level students and researchers of natural resource management, international development and African studies, as well as to NGOs, practitioners and policymakers who recognise the importance of linking natural resources income to human development.

Felix Danso is a Lecturer at the School of Development Management, Ghana Christian University College, and Adjunct Lecturer at the School of Public Services and Governance, and Centre for Regional Integration in Africa, both at the Ghana Institute of Management and Public Administration (GIMPA). He is also an Adjunct Lecturer at the Department of International Relations, Webster University, Ghana Campus, a Council member of the Development Studies Association (DSA) UK, and previously consulted for USAID, West Africa.

Routledge Studies in African Development

The Challenge of Governance in South Sudan
Corruption, Peacebuilding, and Foreign Intervention
Edited by Steven C. Roach and Derrick K. Hudson

African Peacekeeping Training Centres
Socialisation as a Tool for Peace?
Anne Flaspöler

Corporate Governance in Tanzania
Ethics and Accountability at the Crossroads
Peter C. Mhando

Economic Dualism in Zimbabwe
From Colonial Rhodesia to Post-Independence
Daniel B. Ndlela

Rethinking Ownership of Development in Africa
T.D Harper-Shipman

African Environmental Crisis
A History of Science for Development
Gufu Oba

Development in Nigeria
Promise on Hold?
Edlyne Eze Anugwom

Mineral Resource Governance and Human Development in Ghana
Felix Danso

Mineral Resource Governance and Human Development in Ghana

Felix Danso

Routledge
Taylor & Francis Group

LONDON AND NEW YORK

First published 2020
by Routledge
2 Park Square, Milton Park, Abingdon, Oxon OX14 4RN

and by Routledge
52 Vanderbilt Avenue, New York, NY 10017

Routledge is an imprint of the Taylor & Francis Group, an informa business

British Library Cataloguing-in-Publication Data
A catalogue record for this book is available from the British Library

Library of Congress Cataloging-in-Publication Data
Names: Danso, Felix, author.
Title: Mineral resource governance and human
development in Ghana / Felix Danso.
Description: Abingdon, Oxon: New York, NY: Routledge, 2020. |
Series: Routledge studies in African development |
Includes bibliographical references and index. |
Identifiers: LCCN 2020005821 (print) | LCCN 2020005822 (ebook) |
ISBN 9780367437541 (hardback) | ISBN 9781003005537 (ebook)
Subjects: LCSH: Mines and mineral resources–Economic aspects–Ghana. |
Mineral industries–Government policy–Ghana. |
Economic development–Ghana. | Quality of life–Ghana.
Classification: LCC HD9506.G62 D36 2020 (print) |
LCC HD9506.G62 (ebook) | DDC 333.8/5096667–dc23
LC record available at https://lccn.loc.gov/2020005821
LC ebook record available at https://lccn.loc.gov/2020005822

ISBN: 978-0-367-43754-1 (hbk)
ISBN: 978-0-367-50718-3 (pbk)
ISBN:978- 1-003-00553-7(ebk)

Typeset in Times New Roman
by Newgen Publishing UK

Contents

List of illustrations   *vi*
List of abbreviations and acronyms   *vii*

1 Overview of Ghana's mining sector   1

2 Theories and concepts of natural resource governance   17

3 Approach / methodology   46

4 Analyses of mineral resource governance and
  human development in Ghana   53

5 Evaluation of mineral resource governance and
  human development in Ghana   97

6 Human-centred mineral resource governance
  approach   111

Index   *118*

Illustrations

Figures

3.1 Map of the Western Region and its assemblies showing
mineral deposits   48
6.1 Human-centred mineral resource governance approach   112

Tables

1.1 Major mining operations in Ghana   9
1.2 Disbursements of mineral royalties   10
1.3 List of mining sector players   13
4.1 Health facilities in Tarkwa Nsuaem municipality   75

Abbreviations and acronyms

AfDB	African Development Bank
BECE	Basic Education Certificate Examination
CDF	Capital Development Fund
CHPS	Community-Based Health Planning Services
CSOs	Civil Society Organisations
DfID	United Kingdom Department for International Development
EITI	Extractive Industry Transparency Initiative
ERP	Economic Recovery Programme
FDI	foreign direct investment
GDP	gross domestic product
GHS	Ghana cedis
GRA	Ghana Revenue Authority
GSS	Ghana Statistical Service
HIPC	Highly Indebted Poor Countries
IBP	International Budget Project
ICMM	International Council on Mining and Metals
IMF	International Monetary Fund
MDF	Minerals Development Fund
MDGs	Millennium Development Goals
NGOs	Non-Governmental Organisations
NHIS	National Health Insurance Scheme
OECD	Organisation for Economic Co-operation and Development
OPHI	Oxford Poverty and Human Development Initiative
OSI	Open Society Institute
PNDC	Provisional National Defence Council
PRSP	Poverty Reduction Strategy Process
RWI	Revenue Watch Institute
SAP	Structural Adjustment Programme

SDGs	Sustainable Development Goals
SERAC	Social and Economic Rights Action Centre
STMA	Sekondi-Takoradi metropolitan area
UCT	universal cash transfer
UN	United Nations
UNDP	United Nations Development Programme
WACAM	Wassa Association of Communities Affected by Mining

1 Overview of Ghana's mining sector

1.1 Introduction

The notion that mining can contribute positively to the economic and human development of mineral wealth countries makes a lot of sense, especially given the huge revenue mineral wealth developing countries can generate from the sector to alleviate poverty. A country has subsoil assets such as hydrocarbons and minerals, which it seeks to transform into surface assets – human and physical capital – that can be used to support employment and generate economic growth (Venables, 2016). However, in practice, this transformation has proven difficult to achieve. Indeed, few developing economies have been successful with this approach, and economic and social development have generally been lower in resource-rich developing countries than in those without resources. It was not until the 2000s (a period of rising commodity prices) that resource-rich countries grew faster, and even then per capita growth was similar in both groups of countries (International Monetary Fund, 2012).

The World Bank's study of the economies of mining countries between 1990 and 1999 revealed that the per capita gross domestic product (GDP) growth was negative (World Bank, 2003). The term 'resource curse' was coined by Auty (1993) to capture the underperformance of resource-rich economies, drawing attention to the weak performance of countries such as Bolivia, Nigeria and Venezuela, among others. Africa is often said to be a paradox of plenty or suffering from a 'resource curse'. This simply implies that Africa is mineral rich, but the poorest and most conflicted continent in the world. The continent has about '30% of the world's mineral reserves, including 90% of the world's platinum and 40% of its gold' (Southall, 2009, cited in Carmody 2011, p. 15).

Ghana is one of the African countries classified among 53 mineral wealth countries in the world by the International Monetary Fund (IMF) (World Bank, 2011).

Ghana is a West African country with a population of 30,417,856 and GDP growth of 6.3% in 2018 and 8.1% in 2018 (Ghana Statistical Service, 2019). The country is still heavily dependent on agriculture, which provides about 33.5% of employment (World Bank, 2019). Besides agriculture, the mining sector also represents a major sector in the country's economy. The non-oil annual GDP growth rate increased from 4.6% in 2017 to 6.5% in 2018. The increase has been attributed to the 49% growth rate in the mining and quarrying activities (excluding oil and gas), information and communication, and health and social work activities (Ghana Statistical Service, 2019). The country therefore, like many other African countries, abounds in mineral resources concentrated mainly in the southern half of the country, covering about eight out of the sixteen geographical and administrative regions. Ghana's mineral deposits include gold, bauxite, manganese, diamonds, timber, rubber, hydropower, petroleum, silver, salt and limestone. While other natural resources accrue adequate revenue to the country, gold and bauxite alone account for 64% of Ghana's primary exports. Even though there are diverse of minerals available in Ghana, gold is by far the predominant based on recent data (Essah & Andrews, 2016). Aryee (2000), who investigated the mining sector's contribution to the Ghanaian economy using 11 goldmines operating in Ghana between 1996 and 1998, revealed some interesting findings. Over the period, out of a total revenue of US$1.2 billion generated by the mining companies in Ghana, about US$290 million (23%) went into the investment of various parts of the Ghanaian economy (Aryee, 2000). Specifically, it was found that, 'a total of US$79 million was paid as government revenue in respect of required corporate contributions' (corporate income tax, royalties, dividends, customs and excise duties). The most significant of these direct contributions was royalties of US$42 million, followed by dividends of US$19 million and also customs and excise duties of US$17 million (Aryee, 2000). The Western Region is often considered the richest region in the country, in terms of mineral resources, due to the amount and variety of mineral resources found in the area. It is important to note that about 10% of the royalties paid are indirectly redistributed to the local communities through the Minerals Development Fund (MDF) to support the mining companies' developmental efforts in the mining communities. Again, the mining sector employs a relatively significant of the Ghanaian populace. For instance, between 1996 and 1998, the sector employed about 13,000 local staff, contributing a total of US$121 million gross earnings in addition to about US$17 million in Social Security contributions (Akabzaa & Darimani, 2001).

Moreover, according to a Bank of Ghana report for the year 2018, the sector also contributed to the economy through the corollary PAYE contribution of US$25 million, which represented a 9.5% of total national PAYE contributions of US$260 million (Bank of Ghana, 2018). Again, it is shown that over this period, on average, the surveyed companies returned a total of US$571 million (representing 46% of their total revenues) of their foreign currency earnings into the country, largely through the banking system (the Bank of Ghana or other recognised financial institutions) for conversion into the Ghana cedi. This was undoubtedly a significant source of the country's foreign exchange resources (Aryee, 2000).

The sector has also contributed to local content development, where around US$4 million was spent on training staff of the mining companies, with the ultimate goal of transforming the sector towards indigenisation. It is also useful to note that the mining sector has made contributions to the Ghanaian economy either directly or indirectly, which are either 'mandatory, voluntarily through company policy, or moral suasion' (Aryee, 2000).

These kinds of contribution from the sector to the economy still persist. In 2016, an amount of GHS2.3 billion, representing 71% of revenue from minerals, was repatriated to Ghana through the central bank and other commercial banks. This had positive effects on the stability of the local currency and the Bank of Ghana's international resource position. The mining sector's contribution to the Ghana Revenue Authority (GRA) in 2017 amounted to GHS 2.16 billion, which represented a 31% increase over the previous year's GHS1.65 billion. The said amount collected made the sector the highest taxpayer to the GRA in 2017 as it was in 2016. A total of GHS702.4 million was realised as mineral royalty revenue which was also an increase from GHS550.7 million in the previous year (Ghana Revenue Authority, 2018).

The mining sector is also the highest foreign exchange earner for the country. An enormous 4.61 million ounces of gold were exported in 2017, an increase from 3.84 million ounces in 2016. The overall mineral receipts in 2017 accounted for 43% of total merchandise exports. The receipts from gold export were higher than the receipts from cocoa and oil combined. This was because, whereas receipts from export of gold accounted for 43% of all merchandise exported in 2017, receipts from cocoa and oil were 19% and 23% respectively (Ghana Revenue Authority, 2018).

Despite Ghana's mineral wealth, the country continues to face several human development challenges. Human development is a process of expanding the freedoms that people value and have reason to value (Alkire, 2007; Sen, 1999). Both the United Nations Development Programme (UNDP) and the Oxford Poverty and Human Development Initiative (OPHI) uses elements of poverty, such as standard of living, health, education, income levels, empowerment, quality of work and threats of violence to measure the Human Development Index of a country (UNDP, 2014). It is important to note that more than 2.8 million Ghanaians, representing about 10% of the population, are living in extreme poverty (World Poverty Clock, 2018).

It is therefore necessary to provide a balance between mineral resource management and human development in such a way that the management of the resources and the benefits do not come at the expense of human development. As a result, it is essential to conduct a cost–benefit analysis of the industry's operations and to mitigate any negative impacts in order to reap the desired benefits of the industry to human development.

Carmody (2011) observes that mineral resources in Africa have mainly benefited its elites who work in collaboration with foreign interests and international powers. The reasons that explains this situation in the development literature have often been situated in the historical realities of Ghana and other mineral rich sub-Saharan African countries, such as colonial legacies (including bureaucracies and authoritarian rule, centralised command state and international political system of dependence), weak governance and weak institutions, as well as corruption and mismanagement of resource revenues (Todaro & Smith, 2011; Gary, 2009; Pedro, 2005; Pegg, 2006; Allen & Thomas, 2000).

In the same way, a related explanation is that political institutions developed to facilitate mineral resources have been inefficient in their strategies resulting in poor economic performance (Acemoglu & Robinson 2001 and 2012, cited in Lokina & Leiman, 2014, p. 18). The extractive sector tends to be highly capital-intensive, hence in relative terms creating few jobs and few spin-offs.

While recognising these explanations, this book proposes an alternative way to contextualise the issue at hand to ensure that mineral resources are managed responsibly to promote the well-being and quality of life of the people. Thus argued, by strengthening governance and transparency, placing emphasis on reforms in the mining sector's legal and regulatory framework will create an equitable environment for allocation of resources in Ghana and other mineral wealth sub-Saharan

African countries. *Mineral resource governance* refers to the 'set of strategies aimed at improving the transparency and accountability of governments and private companies during the licencing, exploration, contracting, extraction, revenue generation and allocation' (Acosta, 2010, p. 1).

1.2 Historical overview of mineral policies in Ghana

The main objective of all the mining policies adopted by the government of Ghana over the years is to regulate the sector in such a way that the mining sector contributes to the development of the country. Over the past century, Ghana's mineral policy has focused on the mining of gold, manganese, diamonds and bauxite for export.

The late 19th century saw the emergence of the British and other foreign investors who were interested in capital-intensive and large-scale mining (Tsikata, 1997), although some of the local people were into artisan mining before 1941, which was recorded as the period the local people first had contact with the Europeans (Anim, 1994; Garrard, 1989). The mining interest of Britain around the period shaped the formulation and implementation of the first mining policy in the colonial period (Tsikata, 1997). The aims of the colonial mining policy were to:

1. Establish a legal and administrative framework to facilitate such mineral operations;
2. Ensure security of tenure for grantees of mineral rights;
3. Help to manage problems which arose in the relations between mining companies and representatives and members of the local communities; and
   1. Obtain revenue for Government through the levying of duties or income taxes and
   2. Contribute to the self-sufficiency of the British Empire.
      (Bentsi-Enchill, 1986, Graham, 1982,
      cited in Tsikata, 1997, p. 9)

Subsequently, a year after Ghana's attainment of independence in 1958, a Commission of Enquiry was appointed by the government to investigate;

(a) The terms under which [mineral and timber rights] are at present held with the view to determining the consistency of … [the] agreement with equity and with present profitability of these industries and

(b) ... the existence of all unexploited concessions and ascertain when the concessionaries propose to begin working therein.

(Boateng et al., 1961)

The recommendations of the commission after it completed its work in 11 months were that:

1. Government takeover mineral rights from the land owning communities on whose behalf grants had hitherto been made by their chiefs and other local leaders;
2. Royalties to be paid by mining companies be calculated as a percentage of net profit (rather than be fixed amounts whose value diminished with time);
3. Land owners be entitled to a percentage of mining royalties determined by law;
4. More stringent rules be developed to restrict the area over which a mineral right could be held and its duration;
5. Power be given to a government body to terminate a mineral right held for an undue length of time without adequate activity by the grantee;
6. Government investigates the advisability of acquiring 51% of the shares in mining companies and
7. Consideration be given the advisability of establishing as state monopoly for the export of minerals.

(Boateng et al., 1961)

Some of these recommendations informed the Minerals Act 1962 (Act 126). According to Tsikata (1997), in this Act, the ownership of minerals was vested in 'the President on behalf of the Republic and in trust for the people of Ghana'. The president also had the power to demand that minerals produced in Ghana be sold to a state agency at a price negotiated by the High Court. The Minerals Act of 1962 gave the executive more powers to decide on how to use and mange mineral deposit lands, especially those owned by the community, which were presided over by the chiefs, called 'stool lands'. Much of the large-scale mining took place on 'stool land'. The Administration of Lands Act 1962 directed that 'stool land' payments be made to the minister, who would allocate a percentage for 'the maintenance of the ... traditional authority, Projects for the benefit of the people of the area' (Tsikata, 1997). The main policy elements of the Minerals Act of 1962 were maintained through the different political regimes until 1983 when the Provisional National Defence Council (PNDC) launched the Economic

Recovery Programme (ERP) under the guidance of the International Monetary Fund (IMF) as a result of decline in the economic growth by 3.5% in 1981, 6.9% in 1982 and an additional 4.6% in 1983 (Tsikata, 1997). The main objective of the ERP was to remove the various barriers inhibiting the growth of trade and export earnings, which had very important consequences for the mining industry (Hilson, 2003). As a result of that, in 1986 the Ghanaian government introduced the Minerals and Mining Law 1986 (PNDC 153), under this Act, 'minerals in the ground continued to be vested in the state by virtue of the provisions of the PNDC Law 153 and the constitutions' (Tsikata,1997). There was also a general reduction of income tax, and mining operations rates and generous capital allowances were introduced. The main objective of this policy was to minimise the cost of doing mining projects in order to attract investment into the sector.

Apart from the Structural Adjustment Programme (SAP), the PNDC developed a policy of privatisation of state-owned enterprises in the mid-1980s and it was decided to include the state-owned mining companies among those for sale. One of the major reasons for this decision was the losses made by these enterprises and it was hoped that money could be mobilised from the private sector for the rehabilitation of these companies. The privatisation of these formerly state-owned mining companies under the ERP since 1983 has led to phenomenal growth in the mining industry (Aryee, 2000; Addy, 1999; Aryee and Aboagye, 1997; Jonah, 1987). It is worth noting that during this period, 10% of the royalties was channelled to local communities through the MDF to assist the development efforts of mining communities.

The Mineral and Mining Law 1986 (PNDC 153) continued to be the basic legislation governing the mining sector in Ghana during the SAP period (1987–1998) until the current Minerals and Mining Act of 2006 (Act 703), assented on 22 March 2006. This Act was introduced with the objective of making the country's mining sector attractive to investment and promoting development in the country.

1.3 Institutional and legal framework of Ghana's mining sector

Ghana's mineral resource governance is regulated by its mining policies.

The country's large-scale mining companies mainly produce minerals such as gold, bauxite, diamond and manganese, while the small-scale operations produce industrial minerals including limestone, kaolin and silica sand (Minerals Commission, 2010).

It is estimated that gold alone contributes more than 90% of the overall minerals in Ghana and has attracted most of the small-scale operators. Mining operations in Ghana are operated by both foreign and local mining companies. However, the participation of local equity is very minimal, particularly in the large-scale mining operations. Close to 76% of the sector players are foreign companies (KPMG International, 2014).

Table 1.1 shows some of the major mining companies in Ghana and the minerals they produce.

According to the constitution of Ghana, minerals in Ghana belong to the state, irrespective of whether the mineral is found on a private or public land.

The main piece of legislation that deals with the award of licences and leases for the operations of minerals is the Minerals and Mining Act 703 of 2006. One major objective of the Act is to create a friendly environment for investors and position Ghana as a major mining investment destination in Africa. However, the Act has been criticised for its non-transparent, competitive process of awarding mining contracts. As a result, on 20th of March, 2012, a new approach came into being, which requested for tender to mineral rights to be conducted in a transparent and competitive manner. However, not much has been seen in terms of results in promoting transparency and accountability in the tendering process (Adimazoya, 2013). This is because in Ghana's current mining governance system, it is illegal to disclose mining contracts and agreements. In view of this, mining contracts entered into by the government of Ghana and private mining companies are secret documents. Consequently, the Revenue Watch Institute's Transparency Index in the oil and gas mining sector, in its 2010 report placed Ghana 35th out of the 41 natural resource producing countries, citing mainly the lack of access to the contents of mining contracts as one of the setbacks in the county's mining sector.

Adimazoya (2013) has argued that since the mining industry contracts involve resources for the public, and also because mining is a public concern that involves social, economic and environmental issues, the citizens should have access to the content of the contracts.

Apart from the award of licences and leases for the operations of minerals, there is also the structure of the mineral governance system in Ghana. In order to understand the institutional and legal framework of Ghana's mining sector, it is important to identify both the formal and informal governing structures. The local level is comprised of the formal government administration, which consists of district assemblies whose mandate is to oversee the administration of towns and zones. The informal governing structures consist of traditional authorities who are the chiefs, controlling stool lands, which constitute 80%

Table 1.1 Major mining operations in Ghana

Mining company name	Government share	Type of operation	Location in Ghana	Country of origin	Annual output (2013)
Adamus Resources	10%	Gold	Teleku Bokazo and Nkroful (Western Region)	Australia	105,215 ounces
AngloGold Ashanti	1.7%	Gold	Obuasi (Ashanti Region) and Iduapriem (Western Region)	South Africa	239,052 ounces
Chirano Gold Mines	10%	Gold	Chirano (Western Region)	Canada	274,683 ounces
Ghana Bauxite Company	20%	Bauxite	Awaso (Western Region)	China	826,994 tonnes
Ghana Manganese Company	10%	Manganese	Nsuta (Western Region)	Australia	1,997,911 tonnes
Gold Fields Ghana	10%	Gold	Tarkwa and Damang (Western Region)	South Africa	785,421 ounces
Golden Star Resources	10%	Gold	Prestea and Wassa (Western Region)	Canada	330,807 ounces
Newmount Ghana	0	Gold	Kenyasi (Brong Ahafo) and New Abirem (Eastern Region)	USA	699,366 ounces
Perseus Mining (Ghana)	10%	Gold	Ayanfuri (Central Region)	Australia	198,608 ounces
Prestea Sankofa Gold	10%	Gold	Prestea (Western Region)	Ghana	22,853 ounces

Source: Ghana Chamber of Mines (International Council on Mining and Metals, 2015).

of all land in Ghana. There are 95 paramount chiefs in Ghana with most of them in the rural areas of the country where mining activities take place. Standing (2014) writes that mining revenues are paid by the mining companies to the government of Ghana quarterly. Currently, with the introduction of the Minerals and Mining Amendment Act 794 in 2010, which amended aspects of the Minerals and Mining Act 703 of 2006, mining companies pay a mineral royalty flat rate of 5% tax on profits to the government. The mining revenues are paid to the Internal Revenue Service (now Ghana Revenue Authority) which then releases the money into the Consolidated Fund. The distribution of the money is stipulated in the Minerals and Mining Act 703 of 2006 and shown in the Table 1.2.

As shown in the table, 80% of the money is retained by government in the Consolidated Fund and used generally to support the national budget, 10% of the remaining 20% is dispensed into the Mineral Development Fund (MDF) which is mainly used to assist public mining sector institutions and sometimes ad hoc flagship programmes in mining communities. The remaining 10% is quarterly transferred to the office of the Administrator of Stool Lands, which then transfers the money directly to grassroots beneficiaries. The formula used to distribute this money is clearly stipulated in Section 267 (6) of the Minerals and Mining Act of 2006. This section stipulates that 10% is retained by

Table 1.2 Disbursements of mineral royalties

Beneficiary		*Share (%) of Total Amount*
Government in Consolidated Fund		80%
Minerals Development Fund		10%
Office of the Administrator of Stool Lands	10% of Total Amount	
The Administrator of Stool Lands takes 10% of the amount received to cover administrative expenses.		1%
The remaining 90% is distributed as follows.		
District Assemblies	55%	4.95%
Stools	25%	2.25%
Traditional Councils	20%	1.80%
Total		100%

Source: Minerals and Mining ACT 703 (2006).

the office to cater for administrative expenses, with 25% dispensed to the traditional authority to 'maintain the stool', 20% is also dispensed directly to the traditional authority (in most cases the chiefs) with 55% going to the district assemblies located in the area of the authority of the stool land. It must be noted, however, that in some of the district assemblies, the monies dispensed to them can constitute about 40% of their entire budgets. There are no mining revenues available to district assemblies that are outside the jurisdiction of mining areas.

At the central state level, however, as already noted, 80% goes into the Consolidated Fund (a pool of government's resources to support the country's budget).

According to Standing (2014, p. 75), efforts by the state to utilise the mining revenues that it receives for pro-poor development interventions '[take] on heightened significance'. Although part of the MDF has been used for development interventions, Standing (2014) argues that 'the MDF has certainly financed local level projects, including the financing of loans to small scale miners and geological assessments, the total sum of money used for projects explicitly designed for improving local economic development and to compensate for the cost of mining is very small'. A large percentage of the fund's expenditure goes to support capacity building of public institutions that study or work towards regulating. Obviously, this manner of spending revenues from a non-renewable resource such as minerals cannot be said to be a judicious and sustainable investment that will benefit the broad masses of Ghanaians.

Similarly, the International Council on Mining and Metals (ICCM) in 2015 reported that the Environmental Protection Agency – which has the mandate to ensure that the environment is not damaged and that mining is done in an environmentally sustainable way – does not benefit from this payment.

The MDF does not have any legislative instrument to govern its management. As a result, it is unclear how the decision on allocation of funding is made. The MDF has previously received allocation of less than the 10% of mining revenues, payments have been inconsistent and have no separate budget or auditing procedures. The World Bank (2014) in its internal evaluation report noted that the government of Ghana's effort to utilise the country's mineral revenues to promote people-centred development was still a work in progress.

Scholars such as Standing (2014), Pedro (2005), Pegg, (2006) and Allen and Thomas (2000) have argued that this has been mainly caused by the lack of clear legislative policy on how the MDF should be spent, and a lack of transparency and accountability as well as participation in the mineral governance structure of Ghana.

Apart from the state's allocation and utilisation of mineral resources, traditional authorities such as the chiefs also play a critical role in the governance of the mining sector of Ghana. This is because they play a part in the consultation and leasing of land for mining purposes and receive about 45% of mineral revenues dispensed to the grassroots. Although the Minerals and Mining Act 703 of 2006 does not stipulate the role of the chiefs in mining contract negotiations (which is often done by central government), it does indicate the percentage of grassroots mineral revenues that should be allocated to them. Despite the lack of legislation that clearly stipulates how monies that go to the chiefs should be used, it is assumed that it will be used for community development. On the contrary, however, studies by Standing (2014) revealed that too often chiefs have tended not to have interest in investing mineral revenues in the development of the people in their communities. Besides, there are no transparency and accountability mechanisms on how the revenues received by the chiefs are utilised. The lack of community stakeholder engagement and no proper regulation accounts for this (Boachie-Danquah, 2011)

Besides the central and traditional authorities, the district assemblies also play a crucial role in the mineral resource governance in Ghana. Mineral revenues allotted to the district assemblies are also supposed to be used for community development purposes. However, with the current system of the district assemblies, where only two-thirds of assembly members are elected, with the district chief executive appointed by the president, some authors have argued that this system makes the institution vulnerable to political cronyism and patronage (Boachie-Danquah, 2011; Standing, 2014; Debrah, 2009). Previous financial audits in the district assemblies have raised serious financial irregularities including misappropriation of revenues and improper auditing systems, among others (EITI Report, 2016). Similarly, the IMF (2012, p. 101) confirmed in its poverty reduction strategy that 'weak financial management practices is rampant and there is general lack of accountability and transparency in the utilisation of the District Assemblies Common Fund and other resources at the district level'.

1.4 Regulatory institutions in the mining sector of Ghana

The government of Ghana has increasingly since the 1980s privatised the mining sector. As a result, the role of the government has focused on regulating the sector. The institutional framework for the governance of the mining sector is complex. At the state level, it includes the presidency, Parliament, central government ministries, and various state departments and agencies. The Ministry of Lands and Natural Resources through the Minerals Commission, the Geological Survey Department, the Inspectorate Division of Minerals Commission and the Precious Minerals Marketing Company Limited regulates Ghana's mining industry. The Minerals Commission regulates the use of mineral resources and coordinates mineral policies in Ghana. The Geological Surveys Department is responsible for keeping geological information and a repository of geoscientific data. The Inspectorate Division of the Minerals Commission is in charge of monitoring and enforcing health, safety, and environmental standards in mines as spelt out by the mining and mineral laws. The Precious Minerals Marketing Company Limited markets the country's precious minerals and jewellery industry. At the local government level, there are district assemblies and traditional institutions (see Table 1.3).

Apart from government, several other categories of players are involved in Ghana's mining sector. These include non-governmental organisations (NGOs), mining companies, international agencies and

Table 1.3 List of mining sector players

State level	Executive President, Parliament, Judiciary, Ministry of Finance and Economic Planning (MoFEP), Ministry of Lands and Natural Resources, Ministry of Science and Environment (MoSE), Environmental Protection Agency (EPA), Ministry of Local Government and Rural Development (MLGRDE), Office of the Administrator of stool Lands (OASL), Bank of Ghana (BoG), Minerals Commission, Internal Revenue Service (IRS), Ghana Extractive Industries Transparency Initiative (GEITI)
Local level	Fourteen district assemblies that have mineral deposits
Non-state level	National Coalition on Mining, WACAM, TWNG ISODEC, Chamber of Mines
Mining companies	Twenty one mining companies such as Newmont, Ashanti Goldfields, Anglogold Ashanti, Bogoso, Chirano
International players	Bilateral and multilateral institutions the Canadian International Development Agency (CIDA), UK Department for International Development (DfID), World Bank, African Development Bank (AfDB)
Collective players	Citizens constituencies; communities
Traditional authorities	Traditional councils, chiefs

citizens, as well as community and traditional authorities. Eight out of the 13 large-scale mining companies in Ghana are major gold companies. Furthermore, more than 300 small-scale mining companies operate in the country. The mining communities on the other hand are not a formal institution but primary and legitimate stakeholders in terms of representing the areas where the mines are located. The stakeholders have different and sometimes contradictory perspectives on mining issues. To some extent, they play the role of checks and balances on each other, yet tensions continue to exist due to unequal representation and influence on mining sector governance decisions. In particular, there are differences between corporate interests and community interests. Community development in general is particularly on the political agenda, but the government's approach to the poor and other marginalised groups is continually criticised by NGOs. Some NGOs are of the opinion that the state has not developed a culture of community engagement, especially with regard to resource issues. Often, representatives of mining communities have pointed to weak political accountability related to mining. Policymaking is often centralised in national institutions with little or no direct accountability to mining communities or even the district assemblies in mining communities. Generally, Parliament has not been as supportive of mining communities as it could have been.

In conclusion, the mineral governance sector of Ghana lacks transparency, accountability and effective regulation guidelines on how mineral revenues should be utilised. This has led to the misuse and embezzlement of mineral resource revenues. The Minerals and Mining Act 703 of 2006 which is the main legislative policy that governs the mining sector of Ghana is silent on good governance strategies, which affects the effective utilisation of mineral resource revenues.

References

Acosta, M.A. (2010). *Natural resource governance: Review of impact and effectiveness of transparency and accountability initiatives.* Brighton: Institute of Development Studies, University of Sussex.

Addy, S.N. (1999). Ghana: Revival of the mineral sector. *Resource Policy, 24*(4), 229–239.

Adimazoya, T.N. (2013). Staying ahead of the curve: Meeting Ghana's commitment to good governance in the mining sector. *Journal of Energy and Natura Resource Law, 31*(2), 147–170.

Akabzaa, T., & Darimani, A. (2001). *Impact of mining sector investment in Ghana: A study of the Tarkwa mining region.* Draft Report prepared for SAPRI.

Alkire, S. (2007). The missing dimensions of poverty data: Introduction to special issue. *Oxford Development Studies, 35*(4), 347–359.

Allen, T., & Thomas, A. (2000) *Poverty and development into the 21st century*. Oxford: Oxford University Press.

Anim, T.E. (1994). *Gold in Ghana*, 4th edition. Accra: Selwyn Publishers.

Aryee, B.N.A. (2000). *Ghana as a gold producer: The prospects*. Speech presented at Investing in Africa Mining Conference INDABA 2000, Cape Town, South Africa.

Aryee, B.N.A., & Aboagye, J.Y. (1997). Overview of Ghana's minerals mining sector: Past and present. Presented at Mine Consult Seminar.

Auty, R.M. (1993). *Resource-based industrialization: Sowing the oil in eight development countries*. New York: Oxford University Press.

Bank of Ghana (2018). *Monetary policy summary*. Accra: Bank of Ghana.

Boachie-Danquah, N. (2011). *Reducing corruption at the local government level in Ghana: Decentralization in Ghana*. London: Commonwealth Secretariat.

Boateng, K., et al. (1961). *Report of the Commission of Enquiry into Concessions*. Accra: Ghana Government Printer.

Carmody, P. (2011). *The new scramble for Africa*. Cambridge, UK: Polity Press.

Debrah, E. (2009). The economy of regime change in Ghana, 1992–2004. *Ghana Social Science Journal, 5–6*(1–2), 84–113.

EITI Report (2016). *Extractive industry transparency initiative annual report*. Accra: Ministry of Finance.

Essah, M., & Andrews, N. (2016). Linking or de-linking sustainable mining practices and corporate social responsibility? Insights from Ghana. *Resources Policy, 50*, 75–85.

Garrard, T.F. (1989). Gold of Africa: Jewellery and ornaments from Ghana, Cote d'*Ivoire, Mali and Senegal in the collection*. Prestel, Munich: Barbie-Mueller Museum.

Gary, I. (2009). *Ghana's biggest test: Oil's challenge to democratic development* Boston, MA: Oxfam America.

Ghana Revenue Authority (2018). *2017 sectoral revenue collection*. Accra: Ghana Revenue Authority.

Ghana Statistical Service (2013). *Population census report*. Accra: GSS.

Ghana Statistical Service (2019). *Rebased 2013–2018, annual gross domestic product*. Accra: GSS.

Hilson, G. (2003). *Harvesting mineral riches: 1000 years of gold mining in Ghana*. London: Elsevier Science.

International Council on Mining and Metals (2015). Report on mining in Ghana: What future can we expect? London: ICMM.

International Monetary Fund (2012). *Ghana poverty reduction strategy paper*. Washington, DC: International Monetary Fund.

Jonah, S.E. (1987). *The impact of the Economic Recovery Programme on the mining industry in Ghana*. Accra: Minerals Commission.

KPMG International (2014). *Ghana country mining guide*. Amstelveen: KPMG International.

Lokina, R., & Leiman, A. (2014). *Managing resources for sustainable growth and human development in Tanzania: The case of extractive industry*. Dar es Salaam: Economic and Social Research Foundation.

Minerals Commission (2010). *Annual Report for 2009*. Accra: Ghana Minerals Commission.

Minerals and Mining Act 703 (2006). Accra: Minerals Commission of Ghana.

Pedro, A.M.A. (2005). *Mainstreaming mineral wealth in growth and poverty reduction strategies: Sustainable development*. Addis Ababa: Economic Commission for Africa.

Pegg, S. (2006). Mining and poverty reduction: Transforming rhetoric into reality. *Journal of Cleaner Production, 14*, 376–387.

Sen, A. (1999). *Development as freedom*. Boston, MA: Knopf Doubleday.

Standing, A. (2014). Ghana's extractive industries and commodity benefits sharing: The case for cash transfers. *Resource Policy, 40*, 74–82.

Todaro, P.M., & Smith, C.M. (2014). *Economic development*, 11th edition. Harlow: Pearson Education.

Tsikata, F.S. (1997). *The vicissitude of the mineral policies in Ghana*. London: Elsevier Science.

United Nations Development Programme (2014). *Human development report: Sustaining human progress, reducing vulnerabilities and building resilience. Explanatory Notes*. Ghana: UNDP.

Venables, A. J. (2016). Using natural resources for development: Why has it proven so difficult? *Journal of Economic Perspectives, 30*(1), 161–184.

World Bank (2003). *Operations evaluations department project performance assessment report*. Washington, DC: World Bank.

World Bank (2011). *The political economy of the mining sector in Ghana*. Policy research working paper, WPS 5730. Washington, DC: World Bank.

World Bank (2014). *Project performance assessment report*. Washington, DC: World Bank.

World Bank (2019). *The changing nature of work*. Washington, DC: World Bank.

World Poverty Clock (2018). Retrieved from https://worldpoverty.io/

2   Theories and concepts of natural resource governance

2.1 Conceptualising mineral governance

The concept of mineral governance is a new concept that seeks to explain why mineral-rich countries are unable to sustain the well-being of their people.

The term *mineral governance* can be defined as a set of strategies aimed at improving the transparency and accountability in the management of mineral resources (Acosta, 2010). The transparency and accountability initiatives cover areas of licensing, exploration, contracting and extraction, as well as mineral revenue generation and allocation. The relevant stakeholders involved include government (the executive, Parliament and other state institutions), private companies (whose work relates to mining), non-governmental organisations (NGOs), the media and civil society organisations (including community organisations).

Transparency in mineral governance refers to the visibility of decision-making processes in the sector, the clarity with which the reasoning behind decisions is communicated and the ready availability of relevant information about governance and performance in the sector. As a result, it means making decisions about the mining sector and investments accessible to stakeholders and the local people. Transparency in the mining sector is required regarding who has made a decision, the means by which it has been reached and its justification. For example, was the decision made according to the authority conferred on or delegated to an individual or body, according to procedures such as majority-rule voting or consensus, or on the basis of expert opinion, professional judgement and formal decision aids such as multi-criteria analysis or cost–benefit analysis?

Accountability refers to the allocation and acceptance of responsibility for decisions and actions as well as the demonstration of whether and how these responsibilities have been met. Accountability is an issue for mineral governance in contexts where the effectiveness of decision-making processes is essential for their authority and credibility. Where accountability is unrealisable through direct democratic involvement and is more informal, the need of citizens for proper access to information, meaningful consultation, and for enhanced opportunities for active participation become more significant. Compliance with regulatory requirements is an important component of good governance for a public entity. Accountability in the mining sector also requires compliance, which means the extent to which governments and other actors in the mining sector observe relevant legislations, standards and codes and have a compliance programme that is integrated with their operational and financial plans; systems to monitor conformity, such as internal and external audits; and processes to meet external reporting requirements. Reporting requirements should be the minimum necessary to provide financial, governance and performance accountability (Lockwood et al., 2010).

It is important to note that although Acosta's (2010) definition gives an overview of the key concepts of mineral governance, it fails to include other important governance concepts such as participation and equity, which are also essential in mineral governance. Participation refers to opportunities available for stakeholders to be included in and influence decision-making processes and actions in the mining sector. Governance is regarded as inclusive when all those with a stake in the mineral governance processes can engage with them on a basis equal to that provided to all other stakeholders. As solutions to mineral governance challenges often demand substantial changes in practices, their implementation requires participation of as many of the affected actors as possible. It is important for governance actors to have access to many different perspectives and kinds of knowledge, because no single actor has the resources to generate solutions to mineral resource-related problems. Inclusive mineral governance is about governing actors seeking input from multiple sources; having an awareness of and valuing diversity; and having policies and structures to foster stakeholder contributions and engagement.

Moreover, equity is another important mineral governance initiative and refers to the respect and attention given to stakeholders' views, the consistency and absence of personal bias in decision-making, and the consideration given to distribution of costs and benefits of decisions. Those charged with promoting mineral governance arrangements are expected to be fair and equitable in the exercise of the authority conferred on them, particularly in relation to the distribution of power, recognition of diverse values, consideration of current and future generations, and the development of mechanisms to share costs, benefits and responsibilities of decision-making and action. Addressing many mineral resource problems is complicated by confusion regarding who should be responsible for what (Dovers, 2005). Given the cross-cutting nature of such problems, it is especially important to ensure that responsibilities and roles do not fall unfairly on particular actors, such as private interests being expected to shoulder the bulk of the costs for public good outcomes or future generations being burdened with the costs of the present generation's actions. Fairness in mineral resource use also implies practices founded on stewardship of mineral resources for protection of biodiversity and ecological processes.

It is important that the mineral governance structure treats stakeholders with respect and supports their dignity, which is a moral obligation and has the potential to foster acceptance of outcomes. Fair procedures should guarantee that like cases are treated alike, and that where they are irrelevant, the gender, ethnicity, religion, disability and socio-economic status of a person do not determine decision-making processes or outcomes.

Acosta (2010) posits that mineral governance has two main goals: first, it seeks to improve the processes through which stakeholders and institutions can effectively bring governments of mineral-rich countries to account; and second, to effectively contribute to better outcomes, such as helping to improve the socio- economic conditions of people or poverty alleviation. These two goals, although different, are closely related. This is because, when the democratic conditions and practices in the mining sector are enhanced, they will more likely result in better development outcomes.

For these goals to be achieved, problems associated with mineral governance will have to be addressed. These challenges include administration challenges in terms of the necessary qualified staff; informational, infrastructural, technological and financial resources to be able to manage the sector effectively; weak political institutions and civil society organisations, as well as lack of effective policies to ensure that the mining sector benefits local people. These challenges go beyond the executives of governments to include key institutions such as Parliament, mandated state agencies, the security services and the judiciary who are supposed to have oversight responsibilities, support and control over the mining sector.

In order to ameliorate these challenges and promote good governance in the mining sector, mineral wealth countries need to strengthen those institutions that are essential to controlling, directing and overseeing the mining sector. Parliament in particular needs to be given the requisite skills to perform their functions effectively. There is also the need to build the capacities of local community groups and civil society groups to enable them make informed decisions and contribute meaningfully to the governance process. Furthermore, good governance in the mining sector can also be achieved through the enactment of comprehensive mining legal and policy frameworks to regulate the sector while promoting transparency, accountability, participation and equality for development.

Based on the foregoing discussions of mineral resource governance, the following theories will be discussed. They are the rent-seeking government theory, and the revisionist theory.

2.2 Rent-seeking government theory

Mineral-rich countries are more likely to experience less economic growth and increased poverty than non-mineral rich countries (Auty, 1993; Sachs & Warner, 1997). The factors that account for this are several, the extractive sector tends to be highly capital-intensive, hence in relative terms creating few jobs and few spin-off activities. Another factor that is counterproductive to poverty reduction in mineral-rich countries is that, wealth creation often takes place in few business ventures in those countries, leading to higher risks of rent-seeking and corrupt practices among government officials or politicians.

Several discussions on the correlation between natural resources and economic development have often focused on the neglected connection between governance and development.

The main focus of this theory is the often neglected connection between politics and the economy in mostly developing countries. There are three main types of rents identified, namely natural resource rents, rents derived by government intervention to change relative prices and geographical or foreign aid rents (Tollison, 1982). Rosser (2006) also explains that whereas, for example, oil profits, taxes from exports and royalties are economic rents, foreign aid is an example of political rents and rentier states are states or countries that receive considerable and regular amount of rents. According to Auty (2007), three kinds of rents constitute a large percentage of the gross domestic product (GDP) of developing countries, about 15–30% or even more, and as a result of this has the capacity to distort the political economy. The main argument of the rentier state theory is that the recipients freely dispose rents, this is simply because the ruling elites often spend their rents for their own benefit as the state becomes very much involved in the economy. The ruling elites also spend the rents on conspicuous consumption rather than on production. They also entrench and strengthen their positions of power to enable them to access more rents, establishing a clientele state. Apart from this, they further spend the rent on myopic and unsustainable public expenditures. The consequences are weak state institutions and unguaranteed socio-economic development that is not sustainable (Beck, 2007).

Auty (2007, p. 9) hypothesised that:

> [T]he higher the rent/GDP ratio and the more concentrated the rent's deployment upon a handful of political and economic agents, the more likely it is that; (i) the political state is predatory; (ii) the rent is cycled inefficiently through patronage channels and (iii) the economy will lose its underlying comparative advantage. High rents raise the stakes for its capture: capturing such rent offers the elites more immediate reward than using it to promote long term wealth creation, the benefits of which may accrue to successor political and economic actors.

Bevan, Collier and Gunning (1987) and Baldwin (1956) suggest that rents that are often diffusely distributed, such as those from peasant farming, tend to be more effectively deployed than rents concentrated upon economic agents, such as those generated from taxing larger scale capital intensive mines and plantations (Baldwin, 1956; Bevan et al., 1987).

Auty (2007, p. 12) posits that high rent intensifies the 'Olson effect' (Olson, 2000, cited in Auty, 2007, p. 12), which is when ventured interests eventually manipulate economic policies with the aim of diverting the efforts of government, to seize and distribute rent rather using these rents in development interventions that would create broad-base wealth. The continuous dependence on export of primary products has the tendency of delaying competitive industrialisation and also minimises the intake of surplus labour from particularly rural areas. Moreover, Auty (2007) explains that continuous urban unrest may compel governments to create non-market support jobs. Governments also protect the infant industries and extend their bureaucracies which normally expand the rent-seeking sector, slowing down the economic diversification of these countries.

The demands from rent recipient countries eventually increases, exceeding the primary sector's ability to meet these demands, which is normally a consequence of decline in the global price of the primary commodity or structural changes. Governments are compelled to effect economic reforms through promoting markets. By so doing, opportunities for rent-seeking are reduced. This normally attracts strong resistance from the recipients of these rents. As a consequence, governments of high rent economies tend to find it politically expedient to increase the rent generated from the primary commodities, making the primary sector skimp mainly on wages and maintenance. This results in creating a staple trap where as a result of the expansion of the rent dependence the sustainability of the primary sector on which it depends is destroyed. This reduces investments and capital rates, making the economies of these rent-dependent countries vulnerable to external decline shocks.

A collapse of the growth of the economy may eventually lead to a staple trap, which destroys and runs down all forms of capital.

The rentier state theory also proposes the hypothesis that natural resource wealth, especially oil wealth makes states less democratic. Ross's (2001) study revealed quantitatively that 'oil is obstacle to democracy not only in the Middle East region, but that it does harm oil to oil exporters elsewhere' (Ross, 2001, p. 325). Moreover, he makes the assertion that there is lack of democratic pressure on these governments. In substantiating this argument, Ross (2001) advances several causes which could bring this. The rentier state is closely associated with 'rentier effects', which is based on the notion that the ruling political elites can employ rent resources to prevent social pressure by dismantling democratic institutions, and by so doing gain independence from the public. According to Meissner (2010), there are three ways in which this can happen. The first is the 'taxation effect'. With the government getting more money from oil, they are less likely to impose high taxes or sometimes none at all. The public therefore is less likely to demand these governments account for their stewardships, making these governments less responsible to the population ('no representation without taxation'). The 'spending effect' also explains that governments of rentier states often gain legitimisation not by free and fair elections but by buying legitimisation through the use of resources for populist social welfare interventions such as subsidising basic commodities as food, petrol, oil fuel, coal and electricity, and also create more jobs by expanding the public sector. The population oftentimes tends to be ignorant regarding the short-sighted nature of these interventions and policies and how they can dislocate the economy, and often reward these governments by supporting them. This spending effect is targeted at the population as a whole. On the contrary, the 'formation effect' is geared towards independent societal group organisations or movements. The rentier state government often uses its resources to influence their leaders by co-opting or even sometimes buying them. The 'repression effect' is the use of resource revenues by rentier state governments to build up and strengthen the security apparatus with the view of using it as an instrument to supress any democratic aspiration (Ross, 2001, p. 335; Bardt, 2005, p. 7).

While all the above provide logical explanations and reasons for the resource curse, one very important acknowledgement is the lack of a common agreement among scholars on the way forward to overcoming the resource curse.

Moreover, mineral wealth countries have the tendency to experience several negative impacts on good governance. Studies by authors such as Collier and Hoeffler (2000), Sachs and Warner (1997) and Gelb (1988) identify some of the harmful effects.

First, the concept of corruption and natural resources are intertwined. This is because, as Moss and Young (2009, p. 5) have explained, 'many of the resource curse theories use corruption as a key link in their causal chains; others treat corruption as a negative outcome in its own right'. Countries with high rents and other capital-intensive activities provide fertile ground for corruption to breed. This results in a positive correlation between the two variables (Leite & Weidmann, 2002).

Similarly, Gylfason (2001) also finds a strong correlation between natural resource exploration and corruption, and adds that an estimated '15% increase in the share of natural capital in national wealth is correlated with a 20 percentage point drop in the corruption perception index'. Vicente's (2009) study of Sao Tome also revealed that corruption increased by 40% in vote-buying, customs and education.

Second, authoritarianism is the lack of or poor democratic governance. Several studies have found a correlation between authoritarianism and natural resources. A study conducted by Diamond (2008, cited in Moss & Young, 2009) on the 23 oil and gas dependent countries revealed that they were all at some point under authoritarian rule, specifically between 1974 and 2008. This is because most of these countries, if not all of them, are rentier states, they have little need for taxation due to the oil wealth. This prevents them from being accountable to their citizens. In this way, resources are spent to benefit political elites and not the general public.

Third, Moss and Young (2009, p. 5) write that there is a 'robust correlation between natural resources and the likelihood and duration of civil wars', and that several studies have confirmed that dependence on natural resources can be a source of and fuel conflict and lead to the outbreak of civil war compared with other variables such as social fractionalisation and religious or political polarisation.

Besides, Collier and Hoeffler's (2000) model has explained that when export of primary commodities constitutes about 33% of a country's GDP, the potential for conflicts also correspondingly increase to 22%. Furthermore, a country without such primary commodity export has only about a 1% chance of conflict. It must be noted that there is a huge disagreement about the explanation for this in the available literature; however, the correlation remains undisputed.

Fourth, as discussed earlier, several studies have concluded that dependence on natural resources can indeed have negative macroeconomic consequences. This happens because the dependence on natural resources make the economy of these countries vulnerable to external price shocks and further narrows the export base. Dutch disease is one of the theories that explains this situation. Dutch disease was first used to describe Netherland's discovery of oil in the 1970s and how the oil sector attracted labour and capital from all other sectors to the oil boom sector (Corden, 1984, cited in Sachs & Warner, 1997). The crowding-out effect of natural resources is what is likely to cause an economic depression (Sachs & Warner, 1997).

Fifth, several studies have suggested that rent-seeking theory could be viewed as a breakdown of the social contract between the state and the citizens of resource-rich countries. The rentier state does not increase taxes or introduce new ones, thereby reducing its responsibility and accountability to the citizens. An increase in rent means an increase in the incentives of the political elites and civil servants rather than the citizenry in general (Karl, 1997).

Moreover, Moss and Young (2009) have posited that, at the macro level, a decrease in the rule of law is a way of measuring the breakdown of the social contract and tends to be very common in natural resource-dependent countries. Sala-i-Martin and Subramanian (2003) assert that the overall effects of natural resources on the growth of the economy can be attributed to the rule of law. Furthermore, on social services such as education, Gylfason (2001) found a strong negative correlation between dependence on natural resources and secondary school enrolment.

Sixth, it is rational to argue that natural resources wealth should increase income and reduce poverty, however empirical records suggest that the opposite is true (Pegg, 2006). Consequently, from 1960 to 1990, the economies of resource-poor countries grew two to three times faster than rich natural resource-dependent countries (Auty, 2001) Some of the concepts already discussed, such as macroeconomic instability, conflict and corruption, could explain why natural resources could ultimately lead to high poverty rates. Natural resource-rich countries may not invest their resources in development especially through education. This is mainly because there is low demand for highly skilled labour (Gylfason, 2001). In view of that, Mehlum, Moene and Torvik (2006) have also added that there is low investment in human capital, which eventually impoverishes the people. The causalities explanation of the socio-economic deficiencies of governance and rent-seeking theory does not help to understand the non-transformative development of Ghana. Ghana does not solely depend on mineral resources but also on agriculture, and as a result, price volatility of mineral resources in the international market does not necessarily throw the country's economy into disarray. Apart from this, the country's competitive multi-party democracy coupled with its strong media and civil society organisations does not give political elites the unlimited space to abuse mineral rents especially for their personal gains. Since Ghana entered into the fourth republic, political power has rotated between two diametrically opposed political parties, with each succeeding party investigating alleged corruptions and misappropriation of state funds by previous government officials. This serves as some sort of accountability at the political level.

2.3 Revisionist theory of natural resource management

Since the resource curse theory does not reflect the situation in Ghana, it is necessary to discuss an alternative approach. The revisionist theory arose as a direct response to the lower growth theory. Scholars including Ahammad and Clements (1999), Davis (1998), Davis and Tilton (2002) and Goodland (2002) are proponents of this theory. The revisionists argue that the reported negative performances of mineral wealth economies are case-specific and not as general as the lower growth theorists argue. They also establish that the factors that might cause a mineral wealth country to perform poorly economically and socially could be several and mixed. They contend, for example, that a mineral wealth country such as Botswana has a fast-growing economy whereas Zambia is encountering some negative economic growth.

Furthermore, if the mining sector were to be excluded from the economies of these developing countries, their economies would even be lower and worse off. As a result of this, mineral wealth countries can generate economic growth and development provided the wealth is used prudently.

Refuting the arguments of the resource curse theory, the revisionists advance the position that there is no empirical evidence to demonstrate that countries that are mineral-dependent have either slower or faster economic growth. For these scholars, the main problem of mineral wealth developing countries are not economic but political and can be associated with the capacity of government and general society to react to large revenues from mining production. In more instances, these revenues are squandered and not used for productive investments.

The revisionists criticise the lower growth theorists for not offering a workable alternative, assuming that mineral wealth countries would be better off leaving their minerals undiscovered or unexploited.

The challenge of the resource curse has been both theoretical and empirical. The main argument is that the cause of the natural resource curse by mineral dependence is weak institutions rather than the resources per se. This therefore means that the resources themselves are not a problem but the institutions that surround them are the reasons for the curse. Therefore, the concern is with the way the rents from the resources are managed rather than the rents themselves or the resources themselves that create the problem for natural resource-rich dependent countries (UNCTAD, 2013; Brunnschweiler & Bulte, 2008).

Similarly, on the issue of industrialisation and natural resources, Morris, Kaplinsky and Kaplan (2011) have also argued that the weak manufacturing capacity in several resource-dependent countries is the reason for the apparent correlation that exists between weak industrial development and low diversification on one hand and natural resource development.

The revisionist argument holds that there are several countries that have used natural resources as a catalyst to accelerate industrial development. Countries such as Canada, Norway, Australia, the USA, Germany, the UK and Sweden, which are leading world economies, are in fact strongly driven by natural resources and depended on natural resources for their early industrialisation.

Some developing countries such as Botswana, South Africa, Malaysia, Argentina and Indonesia have also benefited from using their natural resources for development (UNECA, 2013; Raines, Turok & Brown, 2001). However, Buur et al. (2013) argue that the extent to which this argument can be applicable to especially African countries depends on the political economy of that country, and that it cannot be deduced from experienced of success stories of developed countries such as the USA, Australia, Canada, Sweden and the UK or some successful countries such as Botswana, South Africa and Indonesia.

While the debate about the causes and effects of the natural resource curse continues, there is a need to focus on the huge untapped natural resource base in Africa. According to the African Development Bank

(AfDB), for example, since 2000, natural resources have contributed to 35% of the growth in the African continent. It also contributed to 80% of the continents exports in 2011 and more than 60% of foreign direct investment (FDI) (African Economic Outlook, 2013). When the agriculture sector is included, then the contribution of natural resources to employment in resource-dependent African countries in 2013 was 50–60%.

In the mining sector, 400,000 jobs (including direct and indirect jobs) have been created by international mining companies (African Economic Outlook, 2013; McMahon & Tracy, 2012). In the sector, an additional six million Africans are employed informally as artisanal miners. Despite the number of people in the sector and the role it is playing to reduce unemployment and poverty, it is yet to receive the needed attention from policymakers (Hilson & Garforth, 2013; Bloch & Owusu, 2012; Nylandsted, Yankson & Fold, 2009; Therkildsen, 2012).

The argument of the resource curse theory may suggest that mineral wealth countries will be better off not mining their minerals. However, as already noted, the revisionists' arguments advocate that mineral 'resources can be exploited and managed to contribute to poverty reduction and growth in Africa' (Pedro, 2005: 13). This argument is premised on the notion that Africa and other non-African mineral wealth countries are endowed with different natural resources of which mineral resources are part. When the natural resources are exploited under conditions that are appropriate, it can spur and accelerate development in mineral dependent countries. Most African FDI have come from the natural resources sector, particularly minerals, oil and gas. Consequently, the mining and oil sector continue to attract the largest sources of earnings from exports.

It is in view of this that Davis and Tilton (2002) have advocated that the question is not whether or not mining should be done, rather the public policy question should be how to ensure that the mining sector is linked with other non-mining sectors to create livelihoods and contribute to poverty reduction as well as the growth of a country's economy and people.

Mineral resource abundance can be harnessed efficiently to drive sustainable development. Economic and social development in the world's affluent countries such as Canada, the USA, Sweden and Australia was fuelled mainly by revenues derived from natural resources. A country's dependence on mineral resources does not necessarily predict that there will be a resource curse.

2.3.1 Governance and natural resource development

Contrary to the view of the resource curse theorists, the revisionists advocate that in order for the booms and busts to be handled by mineral dependent countries, there should be strong institutions, democratic governance that is responsive and technical capacity abundance (Rozner & Gallagher, 2007).

The concept of natural resources can be approached in several ways, which may include a distinction between renewable natural resources (such as forests, water and biodiversity) and non-renewable natural resources (such as metal minerals, including bauxites, gold, diamonds and manganese, and mineral fuels such oil and gas) (Ushie, 2013; Bermudez-Lugo, 2011).

The Organisation for Economic Co-operation and Development (OECD) has defined national resources as:

> natural assets (raw materials) occurring in nature, that can be used for economic production or consumption. These are naturally occurring assets that provide use benefits through the provision of raw materials and energy used in economic activity (or that may provide such benefits one day) and that are subject primarily to quantitative depletion through human use. They are sub divided into four categories: mineral and energy resources, soil resources, water resources and biological resources.
>
> (Ushie, 2013, p. 3)

In the 21st century, natural resource governance has become an integral part of international development both as a discipline of study and practice policies. Governance as a concept has gained global attention among policymakers and been debated on since the mid-1990s. During that period, it became evidently clear that there is a 'vital connection between open democratic and accountable systems of government and respect for human rights and the ability to achieve sustained economic and social development' (OECD/DAC, 1995, p. 5)

Governance as a concept has been defined in various ways. For example, the World Bank defines it as:

> the traditions and institutions by which authority in a country is exercised for the common good. This includes:
> (i) The process by which those in authority are selected, monitored, and replaced

(ii) The capacity of the government to effectively manage its resources and implement sound policies, and

(iii) The respect of citizens and the state for the institutions that govern economic and social interactions among them.

(Kaufmann, Kraay & Mastruzzi, 2010)

In the same way, according to the United Nations Development Programme (UNDP):

> Governance is the system of values, policies and institutions by which a society manages its economic, political and social affairs through interactions within and among the state, civil society and private sector. It is the way a society organizes itself to make and implement decisions – achieving mutual understanding, agreement and action. It comprises the mechanisms and processes for citizens and groups to articulate their interests, mediate their differences and exercise their legal rights and obligations. It is the rules, institutions and practices that set limits and provide incentives for individuals, organizations and firms. Governance, including its social, political and economic dimensions, operates at every level of human enterprise, be it the household, village, municipality, nation, region or globe.
>
> (UNDP Policy Document on Governance for Sustainable Human Development, 2004, p. 6)

Similarly, in the view of the European Commission:

> Governance concerns the state's ability to serve the citizens. It refers to the rules, processes and behaviours by which interests are articulated, resources are managed and power is exercised in society. The way public functions are carried out, public resources are managed and public regulatory powers are exercised is the major issue to be addressed in this context. In spite of its open and broad character, governance is a meaningful and practical concept relating to the very basic aspects of the functioning of any society and political social systems. It can be described as a basic measure of stability and performance of a society. As the concepts of human rights, democratization and democracy, the rule of law, civil society, decentralised power sharing, and sound public administration gain importance and relevance as a society develops into a sophisticated political system, governance evolves into good governance.
>
> (Communication on Governance and Development, October 2003, cited in UNEP, 2013, p. 13)

In the definitions above, the common theme is how society can organise itself and also the kind of relationship that exists between a state and its people. The definition by the UNDP distinguishes three very important spheres in society, namely the state, civil society organisations and the private sector; however, the definitions by the World Bank and the European Commission are more state-oriented. Governance therefore must incorporate these three spheres and other relevant institutions that can facilitate the management of resources of a country for the greater good of its citizenry.

From the above discussion, governance therefore can be described as the processes that are needed to deliver public goods and services. Critical to this process are the mechanisms needed and how they are used to negotiate various interests by different stakeholders in society (Johnson, 1997) and also the processes and tools used for in 'steering of a people's socio-politico-economic development' (Kauzya, 2003, p. 1).

It is governance that balances the utility maximising stakeholder's interest and the interest of society in general. For this balance to be carried out effectively, it involves the establishment of institutions and the creation of mechanisms to enforce and supervise these institutions to work effectively and efficiently (Wunsch, 2000).

Similarly, governance can also be distinguished from government in that the former is broad in nature (which includes a wide range of stakeholders such as actors of government, the civil society as well as the private sector) while the latter is narrow (including the central and local government).

Several donor countries and organisations have made good governance a prerequisite for development aid. In view of this, most if not all of these donor countries and organisations have their own indictors to distinguish good governance from failing governance. However, an overview of the development literature summarises the following indicators for quality governance:

(a) Strong institutions: This includes the existing of formal laws as well as rules and informal institutions such as traditions, norms and codes of conduct;

(b) Participation and voice: This is concerned with consensus orientation.

(c) Accountability: This is related to transparency. It involves accessible information, institutions and processes.

(d) Equity: This relates to the rule of law. The extent to which the governing laws are enforced fairly, laws such as human rights should be applied impartially

(e) Direction: This is about leadership and involves the strategic vision of the leaders. The leaders are to have a long term understanding of the development needs of the people and be able to device strategies to achieve them.

(f) Performance: The institutions and state organizations must respond to the needs of the people as well as be efficient and effective in the use of resources to achieve outcomes.

(UNEP, 2013)

The governance concept started rising in the development debate during the 1990s. Most development authors and donors have argued for good national and local governance as an important prerequisite for sustainable development. Specifically, on local government, Kauzya (2003, p. 1) writes:

> local governance is being promoted in a number of African countries because it is believed that it provides a structural arrangement through which local people and communities with the support from other national, regional as well as international actors can participate in the fight against poverty at close range.

The institutions should be fair and equitable in carrying responsibilities, governance must be familiar to the people being governed and culturally appropriate as well as promote the participation of the relevant stakeholders and offer the mechanisms for resolving conflicts that may arise and provide governance that is practical to the needs of the people (DANIDA, 1999; Kauzya, 2003).

On the issue of actors, good governance promotes the inclusion of all stakeholders, which includes government, civil society and the private sector as well as the local people. Determining who a stakeholder is, the procedures for their selection, what they will do, and how they will do it are all vital for the understanding of governance. The key elements here include promoting broad participation, transparency, legal responsibility and legalising, as well as entrenching and respect for the rule of law.

The overall effects of governance are normally evaluated and measured against the set out goals. The most pivotal question to assess governance effects is what is the extent to which the material and or immaterial goals can be achieved? Goals may not always be explicitly formulated in a way that can be measured and could also vary between different actors (Kauzya, 2003).

According to Siegle (2007, p. 35), '[e]ighty percent of all hydrocarbon-rich countries have autocratic governments. Nearly half of the world's 44 remaining autocracies, in turn, are rich in hydrocarbons or minerals.' It is not accidental that this pattern is occurring, the '[c]ontrol over revenue streams generated by natural resources strengthens the ability of autocratic leaders to feed patronage networks and perpetuate their hold on power, irrespective of the living conditions for the majority of the population' (2007, p. 35) The author argues that livings standards for most people in mineral-rich autocratic countries are worse consistently than other countries with similar income levels.

Therefore, for Siegle (2007), autocracy, poverty, corruption and instability are both defining and perpetuating characteristic of the resource curse.

Furthermore, it has also been argued that as the revenues of mineral wealth countries boom, the autocratic leaders in these countries have less motivation to forge consensus 'with domestic opponents and can behave more brazenly on the international scene' (Siegle, 2007, p. 35 37).

Thomas Friedman describes this situation as the first law of 'petro politics'. Oil prices and the pace of freedom tend to move in entirely different (opposite) directions, specifically in oil dependent countries (Friedman, 2006).

Siegle (2007, p. 35) states that 'on a democracy scale of 0–10, the average hydrocarbon-rich country scores a zero. The global average is 6 ... These differences have enormous consequences on how revenues generated from the mineral resources are used.'

Besides autocracy, social development is another challenge facing mineral wealth countries. For example, Siegle (2007, p. 38) writes that:

> Hydrocarbon-rich countries with per capita incomes between US$1,000 and $2,000 experience an average infant mortality rate of 33 (per 1,000 live births) vs. 28 for the income cohort as a whole, or 20 percent higher. At per capita incomes between $2,000 and $4,000, the rates are 39 and 29 – a third more ... Mineral-rich countries, in contrast, match the global infant mortality medians for each income cohort.

Aside this, mineral wealth countries also lag behind in other social sector indices such as education, healthcare and life expectancy and the people's access to other social amenities. These differences explain the skewed development patterns witnessed in mineral wealth countries as the revenue of the mineral resources accrue to a small fraction of the population, making the majority of the population wallow in abject poverty and making the per capita income figures of these countries very misleading and not speaking to the results on the ground.

In order for development challenges to be addressed, the root cause of governance problems will have to be tackled. This is because that is what perpetuates the dysfunctions of other sectors. According to Siegle (2007), the few mineral wealth countries that have been able to tackle the democratic challenge have benefited while avoiding the negative impacts of the resource curse. Examples are Botswana, Norway, Chile, Mexico and South Africa. The author further argues that 'political competition, popular participation, and oversight of public officials' are essential (2007, p. 38). He further adds that '[t]he more the democratic processes of transparency and public accountability take hold during these transitions, the greater the likelihood that the general population will benefit from resource wealth', but if the democracy is superficial then there is the likelihood of the country suffering the scourges of the resource curse. Siegle underscores the importance of creating democratic institutions, arguing that 'democracies' oversight mechanisms are what contributes most to the consistency and stability of their development performance' (2007, p. 39).

In a similar argument, Collier and Hoeffler (2015) also posit that democracies that have relatively stronger systems of checks and balances are in most cases less susceptible to the negative effects of the natural resource curse, an example being a free press. Media that is independent can play an important role in promoting transparency, investigating corruption and allegations of corruption, holding leaders accountable to their promises and policies, drawing the government's attention to the social challenges of the citizens and increasing adherence to the rule of law (World Bank, 2003; Siegle, 2004)

In view of this, Siegle advocates that the focal point of intervention with autocratic and undemocratic governments is to strengthen institutional checks and balances. He also suggests that '[c]reating controls on corruption, expanding space for the private sector, and strengthening civil service capacity are sensible areas of reform that are generally less than pushing for political rights and civil liberties' (2007, p. 39). This, according to Siegle, will go a long way to militate against the pernicious effects of the resource curse.

There are several strategies for spending natural resources rents in the development literature. Some authors have argued that mineral rents will be better used if all or realistically part of the rents are distributed to the citizens through a system such as the transparent universal cash transfer (UCT) (Moss and Young, 2009). The rationale is that the government will then be able to have the incentive to tax back at least some part of the transfer. Underlying this argument is that it would develop a fiscal contract between the citizens and the government-built mechanisms for accountability and create a responsible constituency for the management of the natural resources (Moss and Young, 2009). This strategy has the tendency to create governments' conventional tax system reliance and may not necessarily generate the benefits that are sometimes derived from direct transfers.

The transfer through pricing strategy is another way. This is especially common in oil producing countries. This kind of transfer works by the government providing cheap fuel policies or providing energies for domestic consumers and citizens of the country through subsidised prices (Gelb and Majerowicz, 2011).

It must be noted, however, that this practice in its extreme form can have serious consequences for a country's growth and development. It could lead to waste in spending, growing consumption and also promote fuel smuggling to neighbouring countries where the prices of fuel are comparatively higher. This can ultimately affect the growth of a country and make sustainability difficult, which in many cases will also make it politically difficult to reverse the policy.

In addition, the transfer through committees strategy explains that rents can be distributed through community-based programmes. A classic example of adopting this strategy is Indonesia, which is building on a long tradition using local action to share public spending through different programmes to the rural areas. These programmes have been successful generally in creating jobs and building infrastructural facilities in the rural areas as well as building the capacity of the local people (Gelb and Majerowicz, 2011).

Another strategy distributes natural resource rents to individuals and households through an institutionalised individual distribution programme. According to Reinikka and Svenson (2007) such distribution, such as cash grants to schools, has revealed the need for high transparency in such programmes to reduce leakages. However, countries such as South Africa have been able to set up a good system of cash transfers, such as child allowances, pension allowances and disability payments among others (Gelb and Majerowicz, 2011). It is important to note, however, that such a scheme cannot be implemented properly without national identity cards.

Critics have argued that the strategy of transferring money will encourage a culture of dependency and may also be wasted by the poor recipients who may not be able to wisely decide how to spend their monies in terms of choosing what is best for them (Gelb and Majerowicz, 2011).

While this may be true, a study by Yanez-Pagans (2008) has also argued that cash transfers can lead to a spending increase in nutrition, health, education and sanitation. This argument is also supported by the United Kingdom Department for International Development (DfID), which claims there is evidence of positive correlation between cash transfers on one side and improved health and education on the side. The DfID (2011) further argues that in some instances cash transfers can increase labour participation by promoting migration and job searches while reducing labour disincentives.

In the view of the revisionist theorists, strong and vibrant democracy with institutions that are well managed in the long run will benefit every aspect of civil life in a country. Therefore, building these effective institutions and promoting a strong and vibrant democracy must be an objective for resource abundant countries battling with the resource curse.

The work of Rozner and Gallagher (2007) proposes three interconnecting and mutually exclusive tools to tackle the resource curse. They argue that for these tools to be sustainable, they must be nurtured constantly since they are not one-off interventions. The tools are participation, transparency and management:

- **Participation:** increasing public involvement in planning for, controlling, and distributing benefits arising from the resource bonanza.
- **Transparency:** improving the transparency of the fiscal sector and ensuring a full accounting of natural resource revenues.
- **Management:** helping government to manage its resource revenues so as to optimize social and economic benefits.

(Rozner & Gallagher, 2007, p. 29)

The three tools must be applied simultaneously. This simultaneous application will create intersection target zones where there are management tools in place, public participation is promoted and transparency also exists.

Countries such as Botswana and Norway are characterised by this overlap and hence have succeeded in overcoming the resource curse (Rozner & Gallagher, 2007).

Mineral wealth countries receive high rents from the mineral resources. As a result, political elites from these countries get attracted to the natural resource rents. According to Rozner and Gallagher (2007), 'participation' is one of the surest ways of preventing these political elites from misappropriating and embezzling the mineral rents. There are three mechanisms to give stronger voice to the public to enable them to be part of the dialogue on natural resource rents. They are '1) fiscal pacts; 2) the Poverty Reduction Strategy; and 3) civil society budget initiatives' (Rozner & Gallagher, 2007, p. 29).

According to Schneider, Lledo and Moore (2004, p. 2), fiscal pacts are 'negotiations (and the agreements derived from them) between organised societal and political interests about public expenditure and how to finance them'. These negotiations are important as they bring fiscal issues forward for discussion.

Guatemala's Pacto Fiscal which was signed in the year 2000 brought different stakeholders together, such as government and the private sector as well as groups of civil society with the aim of developing a proposal on tax and spending that would help the government to implement economic and social reforms that were promised during the country's peace agreement. This was not only intended to deliver tax administration efficiency but also to set objectives and allocate revenues to achieve them and create expenditure for the delivery of social services. Furthermore, the fiscal pacts proposed tax reforms in order to improve public expenditure quantitatively and qualitatively (Rozner & Gallagher, 2007). Rozner and Gallagher further argue that in countries such as Angola, Chad and Azerbaijan, the challenge may not be so much of how to source for money to finance government spending, but how to efficiently and effectively make use of the 'new found surplus'. They posit that in order for resource-dependent countries to have a direction, they must adopt a fiscal pact. The fiscal pact provides direction and steers the agenda of a national policy. The policy could be to reduce poverty, promote economic growth and/or reconstruction. The success of the fiscal pacts is measured by the extent to which the set targets and goals are met (Rozner & Gallagher, 2007).

Similarly to the fiscal pact, the Poverty Reduction Strategy Process (PRSP) provides an opportunity and platform for scrutinising and debating economic policy decisions, making them open and transparent. This concept originated from the World Bank and the International Monetary Fund (IMF) during 1999 and formed the operational basis for concessional lending and debt relief under the Highly Indebted Poor Countries (HIPC) initiative. In preparing the PRSP, the participatory process is used. This involves government, civil society organisations and other domestic stakeholders, international development partners such as the IMF and the World Bank as well as other international donors. They are normally updated annually with year-by-year reports on progress.

The PRSP identifies and describes social, macroeconomic and structural policies as well as interventions through programmes and projects that a country will pursue to reduce and alleviate poverty, promote general growth and well-being as well as external funding (Rozner & Gallagher, 2007). The PRSP creates a platform for civil society and other key stakeholders to get involved at the early stages for priorities to be set to guide government spending. The PRSP is not only needed by countries that need debt relief but can be adopted by resource-rich countries to create a platform for domestic stakeholders and civil society groups to interact with the policymakers and contribute by influencing government spending and investments of a country's mineral resource wealth (Rozner & Gallagher, 2007, p. 31). It must be noted, however, that some critics of the PRSP have argued that participatory process is seldom broad and that in most cases it is limited to a select group in and around the capital city of a country.

Civil society budget groups begun to take root in many countries since the 1990s. Rozner and Gallagher (2007) argue that the civil society budget is especially important in countries with rich mineral resources and where the country's public budgets are mainly funded by revenues from mineral resources. For example, in Nigeria, the Social and Economic Rights Action Centre (SERAC) adopts this method by applying budget analyses with the aim of drawing to the yet-to-be-met needs of the citizens in that country, especially those affected by the exploration of the oil in the Niger Delta.

Furthermore, there is also the Public Finance Monitoring Centre supported by the Open Society Institute (OSI) in Azerbaijan, which was set up in 2003 with the aim of scrutinising the spending of government and proposing innovative ways to use Azerbaijan's oil revenues to achieve the country's economic and social priorities in the medium and long term (Rozner & Gallagher, 2007). According to Rozner and Gallagher (2007, p. 31), the main 'aim of civil society budget work is to translate complex budget numbers into issues that people care about and to lay out policy choices in a way that the public, the media and policy makers can understand and act on'.

The civil society budget group can work at the national, regional and local levels and even at all three levels. The work could be divided so that, for example, while some would be focusing on making the budget simple for popular consumption; others may focus on drawing policymakers' attention to understand the linkages between the budget and policy issues. Others could also build the capacity of NGOs and local community members to serve as 'watchdogs' while some members monitor the budget impact on the social lives of the poor and vulnerable people. Other group members can lobby and advocate for transparency to be deep and accountability to be enhanced during the government budget formulation and implementation.

The Centre on Budget and Policy Priorities has the International Budget Project (IBP), which is an intentional initiative that seeks to support the growth and capacity-building of civil society budget groups in Africa and other least-developed countries. The IBP works by providing technical, networking and financial support to civil society budget groups to build their capacity on how to analyse budgets, and also advocates for budget systems that are transparent and which meet the social needs of the citizens and country.

The IMF Board of Directors adopted an updated Fiscal Transparency Code of Good Practices in 2001 that gives guidelines on how to report and publish information on fiscal matters to member states so as to promote transparency. The coverage of this code includes separating the government sector from the private sector, making information available for the general public, the processes of budgets and standards for fiscal data. There is also a manual that supplements the code to ensure fiscal transparency and governments and other stakeholders can use a questionnaire or survey which comes with the code to access the extent to which the standards in the code are being met (Rozner & Gallagher, 2007, p. 33). Moreover, in 2005, the IMF further adopted the Guide on Resource Revenue Transparency to complement its fiscal transparency guidelines. This additional guide focuses mainly on the placement of the resource rents allocation systems that allocate revenues directly to local and subnational governments, quasi-fiscal institutions of resource-based national firms and debt payments and obligations related to extraction. Governments are mandated by the standards of the IMF to report all operations that are quasi-fiscal to the government finance statistics as part of its overall reporting responsibilities.

The Extractive Industry Transparency Initiative (EITI) is a very important instrument that has the potential to bring greater transparency into revenues from the natural resource sector. The then prime minster of Britain in 2002, Tony Blair, announced the EITI during a World Summit in Johannesburg. The EITI is sponsored and supported by the DfID. The EITI contains guidelines on how to report mining, oil and gas payments by domestic and international companies to governments. The EITI proposes a data aggregation and analyses methods by an independent third party (Rozner & Gallagher, 2007, p. 34). Critics have, however, argued that although the EITI has made some progress, there is still much to be achieved. The protocols, guidelines and other documents that are basic to the initiative are yet to be rectified and have since 2004 yet to issue a quarterly report. Schultz's Citizen's Guide (2005) is another tool for monitoring natural resources rents and how they are spent. Schultz's Citizen's Guide proposes best practices from budget work to civil society leaders that can be adopted to monitor rents from the extractive industry (Rozner & Gallagher, 2007, p. 34).

Furthermore, the Publish What You Pay initiative is another instrument that can be used to enhance transparency. It was launched in the UK by a group of organisations including Transparency International UK, Save the Children UK and the OSI. The main objective of this initiative is to improve transparency in natural resource extraction countries and areas by coaxing oil and mineral companies especially to publish the data on the amounts of mineral rents they pay to governments of host countries. The rationale is to encourage these companies to publish and openly declare all information on payment transactions between them and the government, which include signed contracts, arrangements on revenues and production, royalties payments and other similar transfers to government.

The advantage of this is that civil society organisations and other stakeholders can actually compare what the company publishes with what mineral wealth governments publish. The OSI in June 2006 established the Revenue Watch Institute (RWI), which spearheads and coordinates efforts to enhance transparency and accountability in countries that are resource rich 'by equipping citizens with the information, training, networks, and funding they need to become more effective monitors of government revenue and expenditure' (OSI, cited in Rozner & Gallagher, 2007, p. 32) In order to enhance transparency, the RWI publishes guidebooks, reports and other tools.

Setting up resource funds is a key management tool for natural resource wealth countries. The objective is to stabilise earnings from foreign exchange over time. When there is a boom in the commodity price, revenue is put into the fund so that they are drawn and used when there is a bust or reduction in the commodity price.

Resource funds seek to remove natural resource rents from the public finance system and place them into a safe 'lock box' so as to prevent the political elites and other powerful actors from getting access to them. It therefore means that rent-seekers are prevented from getting access to rents from natural resources (Rozner & Gallagher, 2007, p. 34). Rozner and Gallagher (2007) posit that there have been mixed experiences with resource funds. This is because Norway presents a classical example of how it should work, but Chad providing an example of how an autocratic government can subvert an otherwise well designed resource fund.

Consequently, one other fund that has been used for decades to achieve growth and sustainability is Hartwick's rule from 1977. According to

Lokina and Leiman (2014), the appropriate policy decision to take will depend on the extent of diversification of the economy and how stable its export revenues are. They propose that one way to move towards a diversified economy is by creating a Capital Development Fund (CDF). The idea is that it will direct revenues from minerals towards the development of human capital and the public sector, which are both very important for future sustainable growth and development.

Hartwick's rule argues that for mineral countries to achieve general growth, development and sustainability, rents from minerals should be invested in productive assets and the country should only treat the income on those investments as the country's income.

CDFs have been use in several countries, such as Jamaica and Nigeria. In order for a CDF to be effective, its regulations should be very tight. It is further argued that instead of the fund being used to service recurrent expenditure, such as wage bills of civil servants, it should rather be channelled into infrastructural spending and social development. 'Properly managed such a fund should reduce future bottlenecks as it promotes diversification and skills formation in the economy, and at the same time help sterilize the exchange rate effects of mineral based foreign exchange inflows' (Lokina & Leiman, 2014, p. 32).

Critics have, however, argued that many of the CDFs that have been used across the world have been conspicuously unsuccessful. This has mainly been due to the diversification of mineral revenues into the payment of wage bills instead of developing physical infrastructure and social development (Lokina & Leiman, 2014, p. 32)

On resource funds as a whole, Davis, Ossowski, Daniel and Barnett (2001) have argued that the impact of natural resource funds has been small, especially on the relationship between export and expenditure of government. They affirm that instead of the fund being part of the solution to fiscal challenges of resource revenue boom and bust, they are in fact part of the problem. The authors propose that instead of creating a separate fund, governments should rather address the challenges head-on. This they can do 'by orienting fiscal policy to the long run – maintaining a sustainable non-oil fiscal balance, restraining spending when oil prices rise, transparently presenting the relevant issues to parliament and the public, and potentially hedging oil price risk using financial markets' (Rozner & Gallagher, 2007, p. 33).

Whether a natural resource wealth country will adopt a natural resource fund or the proposal by Davis et al. (2001), there will be the need to take on board 'a multi-year approach to their revenue and expenditure systems'. And this will require some tools of macro fiscal planning to execute this task. These tools are

1. Medium-term macroeconomic frameworks
2. Medium-term fiscal frameworks
3. Medium-term budget frameworks
4. Medium-term expenditure frameworks

All these depict the various layers of budgeting functions and also involve 'forecasting the overall macroeconomy; setting a global budget perspective; developing multiyear revenue forecasts; and establishing budget ceilings for budgetary organizations, programs, and economic classifications of public expenditures' (Rozner & Gallagher, 2007, p. 33).

2.4 Conclusion

There are different theories on natural resources and their relationship with the development of nations. All these views can be broadly categorised into two dominant themes, namely the rent-seeking government theory and the revisionist. These theories generally attempt to explain why mineral wealth countries continue to face challenges with mineral resource management for development.

The rent-seeking government theory's argument is that the poor performance of mineral wealth economies can be attributed to a confluence of factors, including: Dutch disease, which is a situation where the natural resource sector growth crowds out other important sectors of the economy such as agriculture and manufacturing, which negatively affects economic growth; instability and decline in mineral trade; promotion of political elites' interest in mineral rents; lack of local capacity; non-transparent nature of government revenues and foreign exchange; and profligate social, infrastructural and political spending, which even continues when there is decline in mineral revenues and trade. Diametrically opposed to the resource curse theory is the revisionist theory, which argues that the reported negative performances of mineral wealth economies are case-specific and not as general as the lower growth theorists establishes. Furthermore, the factors that might cause a mineral wealth country to perform poorly in socio-economic development could be several and mixed.

References

Acosta, M.A. (2010). *Natural resource governance: Review of impact and effectiveness of transparency and accountability initiatives*. Brighton: Institute of Development Studies, University of Sussex.

African Economic Outlook (2013). Structural *transformation and natural resources*. Tunis: African Development Bank, Development Centre of the Organization for Economic Commission for Africa.

Ahammad, H., & Clements, K. (1999). What does minerals growth mean to western Australia? *Resources Policy, 25*, 1–14.

Auty, R.M. (1993). *Resource-based industrialization: Sowing the oil in eight development countries*. New York: Oxford University Press.

Auty, R.M. (2001). The political economy of resource-driven growth. *European Economic Review, 45*(4–6), 839–846.

Auty, R.M. (2007). *Rent cycling theory, the resource curse and development policy: From curse to cures, a practical perspectives on remedying the resource curse*. Washington: Developing Alternatives.

Baldwin, R.E. (1956). Patterns of development in newly settled regions. *Manchester School of Social and Economic Studies, 24*(2), 161–179.

Bardt, H. (2005). Rohstoffreichtum: Fluch oder Segen? Retrieved from www.iwkoeln.de/fileadmin/publikationen/2005/53806/trends01_05_3.pdf

Bevan, D.L., Collier, P., & Gunning, J.W. (1987). Consequences of a commodity boom in a controlled economy: Accumulation and redistribution in Kenya 1975–83. *World Bank Economic Review, 1*(3), 489–513.

Beck, M. (2007). Der Rentierstaats- Ansatz und das Problem abweichender Falle. *Zeitshrift fur international Beziehungen, 14*(1), 43–70.

Bermudez-Lugo, O. (2011). *The mineral industry of Ghana: 2011 minerals yearbook*. Washington, DC: US Department of the Interior.

Bloch, R., & Owusu, G. (2012). *Linkages in Ghana's global mining industry: Challenging the enclave thesis*. MMCP Discussion Paper. Cape Town: University of Cape Town and the Open University.

Brunnschweiler, C.N., & Bulte, E.H. (2008). The resource curse revisited and revised: A tale of paradoxes and red herrings. *Journal of Environmental Economics and Management, 55*, 248–264.

Buur, L. et al. (2013). Extractive *natural resource development*: Governance: *linkages and aid*. Copenhagen: Danish Institute for International Studies.

Collier, P., & Hoeffler, A. (2000). *Greed and grievance in civil war*. World Bank Policy Research Working Paper No. 2355. Retrieved from http://documents.worldbank.org/curated/en/359271468739530199/pdf/multi-page.pdf

Collier, P., & Hoeffler, A. (2004). Greed and grievance in civil war. *Oxford Economics Papers, 56*, 563–596.

Collier, P., & Hoeffler, A. (2015). *Democracy and resource rents*. Oxford: Global Poverty Research Group.

DANIDA (1999). *Evaluation guidelines: Copenhagen*. Denmark: Ministry of Foreign Affairs.

Davis, G. (1998). The minerals sector, sectoral analysis, and economic. *Development Resources Policy, 24*(4), 217–228.

Davis, G., & Tilton, J.E. (2002). *Should developing countries renounce mining? Perspective on the debate*. Denver, CO: Colorado School of Mines.

Davis, J., Ossowski, R., Daniel, J., & Barnett, S. (2001). Oil funds: Problems posing as solutions? *Finance and Development, 38*(4), 1–6.

DfID (2011). *DfID cash transfers evidence paper*. London: DfID.

Dovers, S. (2005). *Environment and sustainable policy: Creation, implementation, evaluation*. Sydney: Federation Press.

Friedman, T. (2006). The first law of petropolitics. *Foreign Policy* (May–June), 28–36.

Gelb, A. (1998). *Oil windfalls: Blessing or curse?* Oxford: Oxford University Press.

Gelb, A., & Maherowicz, S. (2011). *Oil for Uganda – or Ugandans? Can cash transfers prevent the resource curse?* Working Paper 261. Washington, DC: Centre for Global Development.

Ghana Statistical Service (2013). *Population census report for the Western Region*. Accra: GSS.

Goodland, R. (2002). *How to ensure extractive industries reduce poverty and promote sustainable development*. Discussion paper commissioned by EIR. Retrieved from www.eireview.org

Gylfason, T. (2001). Natural *resources and economic growth*: What is the connection? CESifo Working Paper No. 530.

Hilson, G, & Garforth C. (2013). Everyone now is concentrating on the mining: Drivers and Implications of rural economic transition in the eastern region of Ghana. *Journal of Development Studies, 49*(3), 348–364.

Johnson, I. (1997). *Redefining the concept of governance*. Quebec: Canadian International Development Agency, Political and Social Science Division.

Karl, T. (1997). *The paradox of plenty: Oil booms and petro-states*. Berkeley: University of California Press.

Kaufmann, D., Kraay, A., & Mastruzzi, M. (2010). *The worldwide governance indicators: Methodology and analytical issues*. Retrieved from http://info.worldbank.org/governance/wgi/pdf/WGI.pdf

Kauzya. J.M. (2003). *Local governance capacity building for full-range participation: Concepts, frameworks and experience in African countries*. New York: United Nations.

Leite, C., & Weidmann, J. (2002). Does mother nature corrupt? Natural resources, corruption and economic growth. In G. Abed & S. Gupta (Eds.), *Governance corruption and economic performance* (pp. 156–169). Washington, DC: International Monetary Fund.

Lockwood, M., Davidson, J., Curtis, A., Stratford, E., & Griffith, R. (2010). Governance principles for natural resource management. Society & Natural Resources, *23*(10), 986–1001.

Lokina, R., & Leiman, A. (2014). *Managing resources for sustainable growth and human development in Tanzania: The case of extractive industry*. Dar es Salaam: Economic and Social Research Foundation.

McMahon, G., & Tracy, B. (2012). *Firm and sector-level mining benefits in Zambia*. Washington, DC: World Bank.

Mehlum, H., Moene, K., & Torvik, R. (2006). *Institutions and the resource curse. The Economic Journal, 116*, 1–120.

Meissner, H. (2010). *The resource curse and rentier state in the Caspian region. A need for context analysis*. Hamburg: German Institute of Global and Area Studies.

Moss, T., & Young, L. (2009). Saving Ghana from its oil: The case for Direct Cash Distribution. Centre for Global Development Working Paper 186.

Morris, M., Kaplinsky, R., & Kaplan, D. (2011). *One thing leads to another: Commodities linkages and industrial development – a conceptual overview.* MMCP Discussion Paper. Milton Keynes and Cape Town: Open University and University of Cape Town.

Nylandsted, M., Yankson, P., & Fold, N. (2009). Does FDI create linkages in mining? The case of gold mining in Ghana. In E. Rugraff, D. Sanchez-Ancohea, & A. Summer (Eds.), *Transnational corporations and development policy* (pp. 247–273). London: Palgrave.

OECD/DAC (1995). *Participatory development and good governance.* Development Cooperation Guidelines Series. Retrieved from www.oecd.org/officialdocuments/publicdisplaydocumentpdf/?cote=OCDE/GD(93)191&docLanguage=En

Pedro, A.M.A. (2005). *Mainstreaming mineral wealth in growth and poverty reduction strategies: Sustainable development.* Addis Ababa: Economic Commission for Africa.

Pegg, S. (2006). Mining and poverty reduction: Transforming rhetoric into reality. *Journal of Cleaner Production, 14*, 376–387.

Raines, P., Turok, I., & Brown, R. (2001). Growing global: Foreign direct investment and the internationalization of local suppliers in Scotland. *European Planning Studies, 9*(8), 965–978.

Reinikka, A., & Svensson, J. (2007). *The return from reducing corruption: Evidence from education in Uganda.* Discussion Paper No. DP6363. London: Centre for Economic Policy Research.

Ross, M.L. (2001). Does oil hinder democracy? *World Politics, 53*, 325–361.

Rosser, A. (2006). *The political economy of the resource curse: A literature survey.* Retrieved from www2.ids.ac.uk/gdr/cfs/pdfs/wp 268.pdf

Rozner, S., & Gallagher, M. (2007). Tools for treating the resource curse. *Developing Alternatives, 11*(1), 28–34.

Sachs, J.D., & Warner, A. (1997). *Natural resource abundance and economic growth.* Development Discussion Paper No. 517a. Cambridge, MA: Harvard Institute for International Development, Harvard University.

Sala-i-Martin, X., & Subramanian, A. (2003). Addressing the *natural resource curse*: An illustration from Nigeria. IMF Working Paper, no. WP/03/139. Washington, DC: International Monetary Fund.

Schneider, A., Lledo, V., & Moore, M. (2004). *Social contracts, fiscal pacts and tax reforms in Latin America.* Paper presented for the Inter-American Development Bank. Brighton: Institute of Development Studies.

Siegle, J. (2004). Developing democracy: Democratizers' surprisingly bright development record. *Harvard International Review, 26*(2), 20–25.

Siegle, J. (2007). The governance root of the natural resource curse. *Developing Alternatives, 11*(1), 35–43.

Therkildsen, O. (2012). Continuity and change in Tanzania's ruling coalition: Legacies, crises and weak productive capacity. DIIS Working Paper 2012:06.

Tollison, R.D. (1982). Rent seeking: A survey. *Kyklos, 35*(4), 575–602.

UNCTAD (2013). *Commodities and development report 2013: Global value chain: Investment and trade for development*. Geneva: United Nations.

UNECA (2013). Making the *most* of African's *commodities*: Industrialization for *growth, jobs and economic transformation. Economic report on Africa*. Addis Ababa: United Nations Economic Commission for Africa.

UNEP (2013). *Governance for peace over natural resources: A review of transitions in environmental governance across Africa as a resource for peace building and environmental management in Sudan*. Nairobi: United Nations Environmental Programme.

Ushie, V. (2013). The management and use of natural resources and their potential for economic and social development in the Mediterranean. *IAI Working Papers, 13*, 2280–4331.

Vincente, P.C. (2009). Does oil corrupt? Evidence from a natural experience in West Africa. *Journal of Development Economics*. Retrieved from http://pedrovicente.org/oil.pdf

World Bank (2003). *Ghana: Mining sector rehabilitation project (credit 1921-GH) and Mining Sector Development and Environment Project (credit 2743-GH)*. Project Performance Assessment Report, Operation Evaluations Department.

Wunsch, J.S. (2000). Refounding the African state and local self-governance: The neglected foundation. *The Journal of Modern African Studies, 38*(3), 487–509.

Yanez-Pagans, M. (2008). *Culture and human capital investments: Evidence of an unconditional cash transfer program in Bolivia*. Bonn: IZA Institute of Labour Economics.

3 Approach / methodology

3.1 Introduction

Mineral governance as a strategy to address human development challenges requires the utilisation of multiple data collection methods and analysis. This is primarily due to the fact that human development issues cut across socio-economic, cultural disciplinary and methodological boundaries.

3.2 Methodology

The main methodology of the study is both quantitative and qualitative methods. The nexus between mineral governance and human development requires rigorous analyses and interrogation of stylised theories, facts and hard economic data from official and non-official document sources in order to fully comprehend and articulate the global situation of the subject. It is in view of this that this book hinges on both quantitative and qualitative methodologies to better comprehend the discourse. Qualitative data has been used only to augment the quantitative approach where required, especially in the form of in-depth interviews and observations which are vital research methods of data collection and analysis. The archival research especially on the classified and non-classified documents of both development agencies of state and non-state are key in probing to know the real situation as it is on the ground and can potentially provide policy issues adequate for human development interventions in local communities. Interviews with heads of households and other key informants on human development issues in mining communities provided important and crucial data on mineral governance issues, policies and processes as well as regarding how mining revenues can be managed to promote people-centred development.

Units of analysis are the objects that are being studied in a particular research. This book uses two units of analysis for its research inquiry observation and analysis: heads of households and the nation-state. A household is defined as 'a person or group of persons who live together in the same house or compound, share the same housekeeping arrangements and recognise one person as the head of the household' (Ghana Statistical Service, 2013). The justification for this is that there is a centralised nature of data in Ghana and the decentralised household data. In most cases, subnational data in many developing countries are unavailable and in situations where they are available, they are sometimes inconsistent and incomplete, hence the use of national data. Furthermore, using national data was appropriate for this study since the social, economic, cultural and political conditions found in Ghana are similar to other mineral wealth developing countries, especially mineral wealth countries in sub-Saharan Africa. As a result, findings emanating from the study can inform policy formation in those countries as well. One official each from the Minerals Commission of Ghana, Ghana Chamber of Mines and Wassa Association of Communities Affected by Mining (WACAM) were interviewed in their official capacities. The heads of households were selected for the study due to their position in the household as those who make livelihood decisions for the whole household.

People in the Western Region of Ghana constituted the population for this study. The Western Region of Ghana is the case study area. Data was collected in two municipalities and one metropolitan area namely, Tarkwa Nsuaem, Prestea Huni Valley and Sekondi-Takoradi respectively. Tarkwa Nsuaem and Prestea Huni Valley are municipalities with populations of 90,477 and 159,304 respectively, Sekondi-Takoradi metropolitan area (STMA) has a population of 559,548 (Ghana Statistical Service, 2013). The area was selected on the basis of its mineral resource wealth and socio-economic circumstances, which are similar to the other mining communities in Ghana.

This book specifically employed the stratified, random and purposive sampling methods. The population was initially divided into subgroups called strata and then elements were randomly selected from it. Often it is used when the population of a study is heterogeneous rather than homogeneous. Consequently, this book employs stratified and random sampling methods to ensure that factors such as gender, age, wealth distribution, occupation, different types of residential areas and educational qualifications are properly captured in the sample as they are in the population in order to avoid sampling bias, thus skewed findings. Purposive sampling also helped the study to specifically target and interview key informants whose knowledge and experiences are relevant to the objectives of the study.

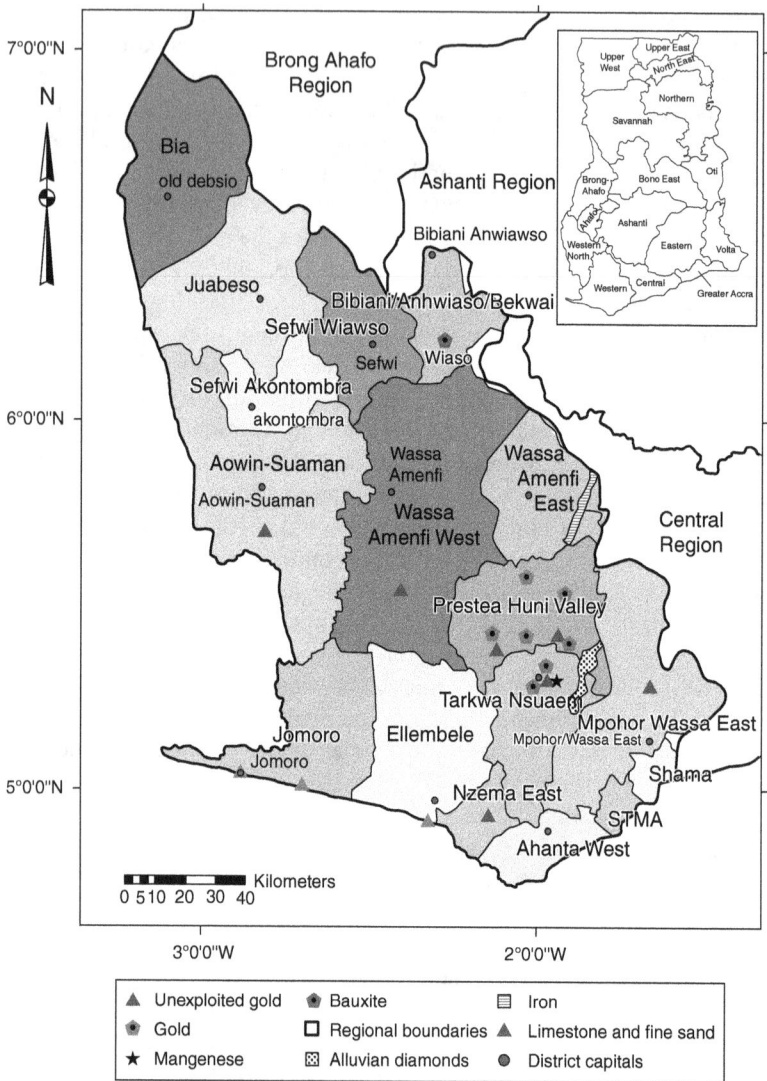

Figure 3.1 Map of the Western Region and its assemblies showing mineral deposits.

Source: Western Regional Coordinating Council.

Size of MDAs (sq. km.)	Location/Coordinates (Lats/Long)
1084.0	Latitudes 40 40′ and 50 20′ North of the Equator and Longitudes 2005′ and 2035′ west
1,809.0	Details not yet available
1,101.6	Latitudes 60N and 60 300 N and Longitudes 20 450 W and 20 150 W.
905.2	Latitude 400′ N and 500 40′ N and Longitudes 10 45′ W and 20 10′ W.
13,758.29	

Figure 3.1 (Continued)

The stratified, random sampling was used to select 100 households for questionnaires. The households were selected from Tarkwa Nsuaem, Prestea Huni Valley and Sekondi-Takoradi. The study selected 30 households from each of the two municipalities, Tarkwa Nsuaem and Prestea Huni Valley, and 40 households from the STMA. The rationale for the selection is that the two municipalities are mining areas with smaller populations, while Sekondi-Takoradi is the regional capital with a bigger population.

As a result of this, 120 questionnaires were administered to the households, while separate interview guides were prepared for each informant and focus group discussion based on the relevant information needed for the study. The 120 questionnaires ensured that the study got 100 returned questionnaires for good analyses and credible findings.

The qualitative method uses three kinds of data collection methods: direct observations, questionnaires and analysis of written documents. This type of research approach, unlike others, is focused on raw data collection so it can explain and interpret the information that is yet to be researched (Patton, 1990, p. 10). This study used both structured and unstructured questions to collect primary data from participants and respondents. Questionnaires are considered necessary to obtain comparable data from all the different respondents, therefore some questions were asked to all the different participants and respondents.

According to Gray (2006), questionnaires as data collection instruments should be carefully formulated and structured and sequential during its construction so that the important data can be obtained in a manner that is most effective. Questionnaires have sets of questions that are fixed in wording and sequential in presentation and also indicate how precisely the questions should be responded to. They must normally guarantee confidentiality, anonymity and privacy of the respondents so as to eliminate victimisation and biases (Bless & Smith, 1995, p. 107). Questionnaires have a list of written questions, the responses to which are given by respondents. Normally the respondents read the questions carefully, interpret them and then write their responses. This instrument is convenient when collecting data on attitudes and perceptions and normally convenient when a researcher wants to collect data that is beyond their physical reach (Leedy, 1985; Bell, 1997). The type and nature of research influences the data collection approach and technique to use. For example, in an instance where respondents may not be comfortable responding or feel reluctant to discuss a subject with a researcher, for reasons such as fear of victimisation, prejudice or discrimination, questionnaires could provide the appropriate means for data collection. Added to this, Tuckman (1997, p. 216) has also argued that questionnaires make it possible to measure a person's feelings, beliefs and attitudes.

This book made use of observations throughout the data collection. Observation technique is a data collection technique that is done through 'direct visual or auditory experience of behaviour' (Monette Sullivan & DeJong, 1990, p. 233). This method was used to complement the other methods of data collection and helped to probe deeply in an informal way to unearth issues to open up new dimensions and areas of mineral governance for sustainable human development. The data that was collected through questionnaires was absorbed according to the study's objectives so as to add meaning to the overall objective of the research.

In addition to that, the study also interviewed one official each from the Minerals Commission of Ghana, the Ghana Chamber of Mines, WACAM (an NGO that advocates for the community development of mining areas) and one mineral resource expert (academic). The justification for this was to get informed input regarding how mineral resources can be used to alleviate poverty.

This book explores multiple sources of data; that is, primary data (sourced from the comprehensive survey using both quantitative and quantitative research methods) and secondary data (data from secondary sources). In the case of the primary data sources, semi-structured questionnaires and in-depth interviews were used to collect data from the heads of households in the Western Region and relevant organisations and government institutions (Minerals Commission of Ghana, Ghana Chamber of Mines, WACAM and an academic expert) respectively. Both closed-ended and open-ended questionnaires were used to collect data from heads of households. Interview guides were used to conduct the in-depth interviews. The reasons behind these instruments are that whereas the closed-ended questionnaires facilitated wider coverage of households, the open-ended questionnaires and interview guides helped to enrich and augment the data obtained by helping to probe further on questions that needed further clarification and capture perceptions as well as attitudes of informants.

Mineral governance and human development do not happen in a policy vacuum, but rather in a set of policy and regulatory structures that administer the socio-economic conditions of development. Important policy statements are mostly found in government policy documents, acts of Parliament and non-state sectorial reports. The book comprehensively relies on some of these documents (such as the Minerals and Mining Act 703 of 2006, UNDP reports, World Bank and IMF reports, Ghana Statistical Service reports, Ghana Chamber of Mines reports and other published and unpublished materials) in analysing critical policy issues as well as consistently following the contribution and performance of the mining sector to the economy of Ghana.

Document review is a logical process of data collection where secondary sources of documents are employed in a study. Reviewing documents provides a record of events over a period of time which is necessary for human development where timelines are important to be acknowledged. This part of document review allowed the study to track key issues from various documents, which has prominently improved the validity and credibility of the findings.

This book employs the state of Ghana as the unit of both data collection and analysis. This has repercussions towards the scale of this research and whether the study did fully saturate the unit. This issue was addressed by analysing documents where a critical content review resulted in an overview of the human development situation in Ghana. Reviewing documents produced data that was explicit and comprehensive as well as free from researcher bias. This book employs document review due to the robustness of data and its high level of precision as compared to human reminiscences of events by respondents.

Nevertheless, it is worth noting that the researcher cautiously scrutinised the documents used for reliability of data, as some government documents could be biased.

3.3 Conclusion

In conclusion, Ghana faces widespread human development challenges. Mineral resources continue to contribute to the revenue generation and foreign exchange earnings of the country. It is therefore imperative for the country's policymakers to utilise these earning judiciously to promote sustainable development. In a study that seeks to investigate and come out with a policy direction for this purpose, there is a need for rigorous methodology to gather data that reflect the true state of the development situation in the country, using the Western Region as a case to put the critical issues of mineral resources and development to the fore. Investing in education, health and the general standard of living of the people should be at the core of government policy in the utilisation of mineral earnings. Stimulating and securing sustainable livelihoods of the millions of Ghanaians in the aforementioned areas should be enough impetus for the state to redefine the terms of its development interventions. In view of this, the book utilised the mixed methods to probe the socio-economic conditions of Ghanaians. Relying on both quantitative and qualitative methods of data collection, the key issues of human development are captured.

References

Bell, J. (1997). *Doing your research project: A guide for first-time researchers in education, health and social science.* Milton Keynes: Open University Press.
Bless, C., & Smith, C.H. (1995). *Fundamentals of social research methods: An African perspective*, 2nd edition. Cape Town: Juta.
Ghana Statistical Service (2013). *Population census report.* Accra: GSS.
Gray, D. (2006). *Doing research in the real world.* London: Sage.
Leedy, P.D. (1985). *Practical research: Planning and design.* New York: Palgrave Macmillan.
Minerals and Mining Act 703 (2006). Accra: Minerals Commission of Ghana.
Monette, D.R., Sullivan, T.J., & DeJong, C.R. (1990). *Applied social research: A tool for the human services*, 2nd edition. Marquette, MI: Northern Michigan University Press.
Patton, M. (1990). *Qualitative evaluation and research methods.* Thousand Oaks, CA: Sage.
Tucker, B.W. (1997). *Conducting educational research.* New York: Harcourt Brace.

4 Analyses of mineral resource governance and human development in Ghana

4.1 Introduction

Structuring the mineral governance system in Ghana to promote socio-economic development continues to be a major concern for development managers and theorists alike. Weak and ineffective mineral governance system often result in irresponsible mining and misuse of mineral rents, which can be detrimental to the livelihoods of the people living in the mining regions and communities. This chapter describes the extent, nature and effects of mineral rents on the socio-economic development of Ghana with specific focus on the Western Region. Field data was collected from two municipalities and one metropolitan area, namely Tarkwa Nsuaem, Prestea Huni Valley and Sekondi-Takoradi respectively. The chapter starts by analysing the household demographic information with the view to understanding the major characteristics of the respondents. This is preceded by analyses of the well-being of household members and their housing characteristics, which gives an idea of their standard of living and their coping strategies for their livelihoods. Further analyses of education and access to medical care in the Western Region are also presented in this chapter. This is followed by analyses of the job opportunities that mining provides. Equally essential is transparency and accountability in the mining sector. In view of this, analyses of transparency and accountability on the mineral governance sector are also presented. In order to promote inclusive development in the mining sector, the chapter also analyses the extent to which the mining sector promotes equitable participation of especially vulnerable persons of Ghanaian society in relation to employment opportunities in the mining sector.

4.2 Household demographic information

4.2.1 The structure of households

Households are very important units in development planning and management. Social interventions often target households, especially in the delivery of goods and services. As a result, in a study of mineral governance and its linkages to human development in Ghana and sub-Saharan Africa, knowledge of the structure, composition and headship of households provides statistical and descriptive details for socio-economic analyses and policy considerations. Families mainly constitute households in both rural and urban Ghana. The role of the family in Africa is very crucial. Nukunya (2003, p. 50) observes that in Africa the functions of the family may be listed as procreation, socialisation and economic cooperation. There are two types of family ties that inform the formation of households in Africa, the nuclear and the extended systems of family. The nuclear family system comprises the father, mother and their unmarried children (usually biological and/or adopted). On the other hand, the extended family comprises the nuclear family, parents, siblings and other relatives, either built around the patrilineal or matrilineal family (in most cases but not both) (Nukunya, 2003). Patrilineal families are those built around a common ancestor (male) whereas matrilineal systems of family organisation are built around a common ancestress (female). In Ghana, both forms of family systems exist and may constitute a household. This makes the concept of a family closely linked with that of a household in terms of their formation. However, whereas families are groups of people related by ties of consanguinity, marriage or adoption, in household formation and definition, members are not necessarily related by ties of consanguinity but rather they live together to constitute a single consumption unit (Nukunya, 2003).

In order to understand the characteristics of a country or region's population, it is fundamental to understand the dynamics of its households. This is because the characteristics of a country or region's households is a reflection of the entire population of the country. This therefore makes the households very important units of analysis for local, regional and national contexts because local economic activity is vertically integrated into the national system.

A traditional Ghanaian household comprises the head of the household, children, in-laws, siblings, other relatives and non-relatives (Ghana Statistical Service (GSS), 2013). This places the majority of such households into the extended family category. The head of household has varying definitions across countries, regions and continents. However, for the purposes of this study, the head of a household is defined as:

> a member of the household who is recognised as such by the other members of the household. The head of the household is generally the person who has the economic and social responsibility for the household. All relationships are defined with reference to the head.
>
> (GSS, 2013, p. 69)

The head of the household therefore refers to the breadwinner (male or female), the one who makes decisions for the household while other members recognise them as such. This study targeted the heads of household and shows the distribution of the gender of the respondents and indicates that 97 out of the 100 respondents indicated their gender. Out of field data collected, the male respondents constitute 75% of the heads of household while the female respondents constitute 22%.

Out of the 100 respondents, 96 of them responded to the question of who the head of the household is. The study revealed that 63% of the households are headed by a husband, 13% headed by a wife, 6% headed by a son, 1% headed by a daughter, 4% by a brother, 3% by an uncle and 6% by other members who are not in any of the categories mentioned. This means that majority of the heads of households in this study are males.

In most of the cases, the husband is regarded as the head of the household. This reflects the dominance of men over women in the households in terms of authority and also being the breadwinner. The nature of dominance by men is seen in areas such as household decision-making and property ownership. This reflects the nature of traditional African communities where males are perceived as heads of households regardless of their statuses and that of their wives. This subscribes to the patriarchal view that men are mainly providers to the families whereas women are assigned to household chores. This assertion is also evident in the considerable number of households headed by husbands, brothers, sons and uncles.

Consequently, in many African cultures, a woman who is widowed, separated or divorced by her husband is normally not left on her own. As a result of this, many cultures put in place a support system to take care of these women. They are in most cases taken care of by their adult son, an uncle or a brother from her natal home. In some instances, where women are seen as potential household heads, the headship position is often assigned to men. In recent times, however, there have been an emergence of households headed by women due to increasing social stress created by the prevailing economic conditions and unavailability of males in the family due to factors such as migration, divorce, male deaths and disruption in the family leading to a shift from the male-dominated household headship.

4.2.2 Age of household heads

Age helps to understand an individual's personality make up, preferences, needs and their ability to make decisions, which are linked to a person's experience, skills and knowledge to address challenges. This knowledge is also very important in contributing to household income and helping to improve the standard of living even of the poorest in society. The respondents of the study were asked to indicate their ages. For the purposes of analysis, the ages of the heads of households were divided into four categories, namely, 18–30 years, 31–45 years, 46–60 years and 61–75 years. Out of the 100 respondents, 98 of them responded to the question of what their ages were.

From their responses, 3% were aged 18–30 years, 45% were aged 31–45, 38% were aged 46–60 years and 11% were aged 61–75 years. Only 1% of the respondents were above 75 years. From the results, the economically productive ages (18–60) constitute 86% of the respondents. This means that majority of the respondents are economically active members of the population. Whether in job creation, education, health and other social services, these economically active members of the society are likely to take advantage of these opportunities to benefit themselves and other members of their households. The percentage of the respondents considered as economically inactive (61–75) are 11%. These people may not be able take advantage of job creation opportunities in the mining sector by themselves, but can, however, access other development opportunities the mining sector can bring, such as in the health sector.

4.2.3 Marital status of household heads

In traditional Ghanaian society, it is very unusual for men or women to decide to stay single throughout their life. Every person is expected to marry. The definition of marriage in the Ghanaian traditional society is clearly captured by Nukunya (2003, p. 43) who stated that 'marriage is a union in which the couple has gone through the procedures recognised in the society for the purposes of sexual intercourse, raising of a family or companionship'. Marriage in Ghana is a union not just between the two spouses, but their families as well.

As a result, it is incumbent on members of both families to ensure that they support the couple in every way possible to have a successful marriage. These supports include economic support, socialising children born out of the wedlock and helping to resolve conflict that may arise between the couple.

The marital status of household heads is a crucial indicator that can be used to predict a wide range of socio-economic outcomes. All things being equal, if the two parents are present, they can provide favourable and acceptable conditions for the children and other members of the household, as the two can collectively or individually provide the psychological, socio-emotional and environmental materials needed by members of the family for their support and well-being. In view of this, the respondents were asked to indicate their marital statuses. The marital status of the respondents was divided into married, single, divorced, separated and widowed.

From the field data, 99 out of the 100 respondents expressed their opinions on this question. Out of this, 71% of them were married, 11% were single, 5% divorced, 7% separated and 5% widowed. Thus, 28% of the respondents are single household heads with the majority being married heads of households. This trend is in line with Ghana Statistical Service report (GSS, 2013, p. 84), which indicates that 'currently married household heads constituted the largest proportion in both urban and rural areas'. The proportion of single heads of household is not very significant. Perhaps reasons for their singleness could be economic, such as lack of money to pay the bride price especially on the part of the males, or that they are waiting to meet their preferred partners. Consequently, the Ghanaian cultures insist on the payment of the bride price and the procedures for the marriage as essential elements in the marriage definition. As a result, some of the respondents may be labelled single when indeed they may be cohabiting with their partners. Some people choose cohabitation as a test drive for a relationship before marriage. A small percentage of them responded that they were divorced (5%). The low divorce rate could be as a result of the many marriages being contracted through strong customary and religious rites.

4.2.4 Types of marriage

Marriage types, roles and characteristics differ from culture to culture and are also dynamic over time. The study categorised marriages into three types, namely civil marriages, registered customary marriages and unregistered customary marriages. Out of the 100 respondents,

72 of them responded to their type of marriages. From the responses, registered customary marriages recorded the highest respondents with 36%, unregistered customary marriages recorded 25% with civil marriages recording 11%.

The field data indicates that majority of the respondents are married under the customary marriages (both registered and unregistered) constituting 61% of the respondents.

In many Ghanaian societies, customary elements have tended to precede modern types of marriages such as ordinance marriages in which the union is registered at the Registrar General's Department or the office of a City Council, and Christian or church marriage in which the union is consecrated by a priest or minister of a church (Assimeng, 1999; Nukunya, 2003). This is so because, in Ghanaian culture, marriage is not just a union between individuals, but families, and the customary marriage provides the traditional platform for this purpose. Customary marriages are not legal unless registered, but are seen as conforming to society's acknowledged standards. The non-recognition of customary marriages can sometimes bring hardship to the children born out of such marriages, as they may be seen as illegitimate children. This is because wives from civil marriages are regarded as legitimate and sometimes are not given the same status as those from customary marriages. Civil and registered customary marriages enjoy the full protection of the law and are regarded as legal unions.

4.2.5 Religion of respondents

Ghana's 1992 Republican constitution guarantees freedom of religion and worship. This study asked the heads of the households to indicate their religious affiliations. The religious affiliation was categorised into Christian, Muslim and other religions. Out of the 100 respondents, 99 responded to the question of their religious affiliation. The field data revealed that Christians constituted 94% of the respondents, Muslims constituted 3%, with nobody as a traditional believer, and 2% as members of other religions, usually Eastern religions such as Buddhism, hinduism, shintoism and Eckankar (a modern religion), which are currently gaining grounds in the country.

From the field data, a vast majority of the respondents are Christians which confirms the report of the GSS (2013, p. 63) which revealed that 71.2% of the respondents were Christians followed by Muslims constituting 17.6%, and 5.2% who were traditional African believers.

4.2.6 *Level of education of heads of households*

Level of education refers to the highest level of formal school attended by a person or which a person is currently attending. Education is an essential tool that provides people with the requisite knowledge skills for better employment opportunities and quality of life. Education is closely associated with human development of a people (UNDP, 2011) and as a result, one of the aims of this study. Respondents were asked to indicate their level of education. There were six categories under the level of education namely no formal education, primary education, junior high school/ junior secondary school/middle school, senior secondary school, tertiary education and other levels. Respondents who answered to this question were 92 out of the 100. Those with no formal education constituted 5%, while 1% had primary education. Junior high/junior secondary/middle school respondents constituted 37%, with senior secondary leavers at 12%. Respondents with tertiary education constituted 36% and 1% have other forms of education. The illiteracy rate is low since 5% have no formal education, signifying that majority of the respondents are literate.

The higher the educational level of a person, the more the person is likely to get access to other development opportunities that the mining sector may bring, such as education and other social opportunities. In terms of job opportunities, education can lead to a person being employed directly by a mining company or other indirect job opportunities in the mining chain. Education can also equip a person with the capacity to search for information and read what is going on, thereby helping one to be in a better position to insist on his/her rights. In the mining communities, rights such as livelihood rights, environmental sustainability, the need to demand accountability and transparency from their leaders as well as general provision of social services can be enhanced by high literacy rates.

4.2.7 *Household size*

Household size refers to the total number of people in a household regardless of age, sex or residential status (GSS, 2013, p. 70). Household size in this study is measured by the number of persons residing in a single house and sharing the same resources. These people may or may not be related by ties of consanguinity but normally live and eat together. The size of the household was categorised as follows: 1–3 members, 4–6 members, 7–9 members and 10–12 members. The field data presents that majority of the households, 58%, were in the category

4–6 persons. This was followed by 1–3 members recording 38%, and 4% for 7–9 persons with no household in the category of 10–12 persons.

According to the GSS (2013), the average (mean) size of a household in Ghana in the 2000 national census was 5.1 persons, which declined to 4.4 persons in the 2010 census. This therefore means that majority of the household size in this study (4–6 persons) is the same category as the national average in the 2010 national census. Large household sizes (seven persons and above) may be mainly due to the extended family of many African societies. However, factors such as education, urbanisation, family planning and high cost of living could also be contributing to small household sizes.

4.2.8 Composition of households

The composition of a household is crucial in analysing the socio-economic well-being of household members in that it helps to determine the dependency ratio of these households. Respondents were asked to indicate the composition of their households in terms of male adults, female adults, male children and female children. The field data gives the distribution of their responses and indicates that 94 out of the 100 respondents responded to this question.

The study revealed that 43% constituted male adults in the households selected for the study while 28% constituted female adults in the households selected. The proportion of male children constitutes 10% with 13% representing female children. This means that out of the households selected for the study, 71% of the household members are adults with 23% being children in the households selected for the study.

4.2.9 Occupation of household heads

Broadly defining, occupation focuses on the various kinds of economic activities people engage in for their livelihood. Occupation of a person gives an idea of their social status and therefore their socio-economic well-being. The heads of the households were to indicate their occupations. Out of the 100 respondents, 95 responded to this question. The study categorised the occupation of the respondents into: professional/technical/managerial, sales/services, agriculture, manual work, people who are unemployed, pensioners and other occupations not captured in the categories mentioned. The field data presents that 44% of the respondents were in the professional/technical/managerial category, the sales/services sector constituted 24%, the agricultural sector constituted 2%, 17% were in manual work, 2% were unemployed, 4%

were pensioners and 2% fell in other categories not captured in any of the above.

With 44% of the respondents in the professional/technical/managerial sector, it means that many of the household heads have some skills or professional training. Again, as in many mining towns, the sales (retail) and services sector employs quite a large number of people due to the boost in the sector resulting from the mining activities. Some unskilled opportunities are also created in the area as well. Generally, however, unemployment is rather on the low side with only 2% in the category. This trend could be that, perhaps due to the high cost of living, almost everyone tries to find some work to do so as to make a living. However, agriculture, which is the mainstay of the Ghanaian economy, only employs 2% of the respondents. The reason for this situation could be several; however, the most obvious one could be that many people are attracted to the mining sector and its related activities to the detriment of the agricultural sector. This situation is prevalent in mining communities, whereas agriculture continues to be the main occupation of people in non-mining communities.

4.2.10 Household sources of income and annual income

The respondents were asked to indicate their sources of income and their annual income estimates. In Ghana, just like many other countries, the main source of income for many people is often from their main occupation. The sources of income had the following categories: farming, pension, remittances, government, self-job and others. Out of the respondents, 99% responded to this question.

The field data indicates that respondents who get their sources of income from government constituted 43%, those from self-job (private jobs) constituted 42%, with 7% from pension sources, 1% from farming, 1% from remittances and 5% from other sources.

Furthermore, the respondents were made to state their annual range of income. The Ghanaian cedi was used to measure the income of the heads of households. The currency is, however, weak against the US dollar, with one US dollar equivalent to about 3.95 Ghanaian cedis. The field data shows the annual income of the interviewed respondents. The Ghanaian currency symbol (GHS) is used. Of the respondents, 30% earn less than GHS2,500, 28% earn GHS2,501–3,500, 5% earn GHS3,501–4,500, 3% earn GHS4,501–5,500 and 34% did not respond to the question.

The response indicates that majority of the respondents earns GHS3,500 or less annually, which is equivalent to US$886.07.

Internationally, the World Bank considers a person living below US$1.9 per day (approximately US$693.5 per annum as poor, since they are living below the poverty line. Such poverty translates into high cost of living or unaffordability of certain basic needs such as food, transport, clothing, education and healthcare. With low unemployment levels, a poor standard of living could be explained by low-income earning from their various jobs.

4.3 Housing conditions and well-being of household members

This section analyses the housing conditions and well-being of the household members in the three districts selected for the study.

4.3.1 Type of house

The United Nations (UN, 2008, p. 9) defines a house as 'structurally separate and independent place of abode such that a person or group of persons can isolate themselves from the hazards of climate such as storms and the sun'. This therefore means that a house is an independent and structurally separate place of living for people. The most important characteristics are the separateness and independence. An enclosure could be considered as separate provided it is surrounded by fences, walls and other conducive materials such that a person or group of persons will be separated from others in the community for purposes such as sleeping, cooking and eating as well as protecting themselves from climate hazards such as severe wind and rainfall. The study's definition of house covered separate houses, semi-detached houses, compound houses, kiosks/containers/improvised homes and uncompleted buildings. The study asked the respondents to indicate the type of houses they live in.

The field data gives the distribution of their responses and shows that 96 of the respondents out of the 100 responded to this question. The study revealed that 10% of the respondents live in separate houses, 25% in semi-detached houses, 1% in kiosk/container/improvised houses and 2% in uncompleted houses. A narrow majority of the respondents constituting 58% live in compound houses, which are houses with different households occupying different rooms. This form of household is the most common type of household in Ghana. In Ghana's 2010 national census, the GSS (2013, p. 376) reported that 'at both the national and regional levels, the compound houses were the most common form of dwelling unit accounting for more than one-half of the total of houses'. All things being equal, a household's housing type can be used to determine the standard of living of the household. The reason being that households with very low standards of living often live in compound houses whereas separate and semi-detached houses are occupied by households with relatively high standards of living. Kiosk/containers/ improvised houses are often occupied by poor households because most of them will not be able to afford the cost of renting a house.

4.3.2 Number of rooms

According to the GSS (2013, p. 376) a room is defined as 'a space in the housing unit or other living quarters enclosed by walls reaching from the floor to the ceiling or roof covering, or at least to a height of two metres, of a size large enough to hold a bed for an adult, that is at least four square meters'. The study adopted this definition because it reflects the nature of rooms in Ghana. The number of rooms of a household can also determine the standard of living of the household. There is also a correlation between household income size and the number of rooms in the household, in relation to the size of the household. The respondents of the study were made to indicate the number of rooms in their households. Out of the 100 respondents, 88 of them responded to this question. The field data gives a breakdown of their responses. The majority of the respondents, representing 77% of the households selected for the study, have 1–4 rooms, the number of households with 5–10 constitutes 5%, with 6% having more than five rooms.

4.3.3 Occupancy status of household heads

The field data also revealed the holding arrangements and tenure of the units of dwelling among the respondents. Four major types of tenures exist in Ghana, namely renting, rent-free, owner-occupier and perching. 'Perching' is a borrowed English term, meaning someone who is neither living in a house as owner nor renting. Such people are only occupying a small space due to financial challenges. Out of the 95% that responded, the proportion of households that falls into the category of owner-occupier is 13%, 16% of the respondents indicated that their occupancy status is rent-free, those renting constitute 65%, with 1% perching. The majority of the dwelling units are rented properties.

4.3.4 Connection to electricity

The nature of the power source is one of the crucial indicators for assessing the quality of life of a people and has nowadays become a human right. Improvements in society shift the source of lighting from low-quality sources, which include firewood, to electricity, which is a more efficient source. The field data gives the distribution of the main sources of electricity connection for the selected households for the study.

The field data indicates that the main source of electricity connection is the national electricity grid, with a vast majority of 92% of households connected to it, with only 7% not connected. This implies that the Western Region is not different from other parts of the Ghana in terms of electricity connection to the national grid.

Accordingly, the GSS (2013) identified the main sources of lighting for households as electricity (grid), kerosene lamp and candles/torches. However, recently, there has been the introduction of solar energy sources for households.

The field data shows the sources of lighting for the interviewed households. From the data, the main source of lighting for the interviewed households is the electricity (grid), which constitutes 89%, followed by candles and torches, which constitute 6%, with only 1% without electricity.

Respondents were further asked to indicate how regular their main power supply was after sunset. Regular electricity supply is essential for the development of every society. The field data shows the distribution of their responses. Out of the 100 respondents interviewed, 88 of them responded to this question.

From the field data, the respondents were made to select from the options provided and shows that 19% indicated that they have regular power supply, 16% responded that they experienced power cuts more than twice a week. The proportion of the respondents who indicated that they experienced power cuts once or twice in a week constituted a narrow majority of 51%, with 2% indicating that their option is not captured in any of the categories.

Furthermore, equally important on the issue of lighting is the availability of street lights, and it is one of the ways of determining the standard of social amenities in a community. In Ghana, the unavailability of streetlights is not just a common feature of rural areas but also of urban areas. The respondents were asked to indicate whether they have street lights in their communities. Out of the 100 respondents, 97 responded to this question. The majority constituting 87% of the respondents, indicated that they have street lights in their communities, 10% indicated that they do not have street lights in their communities.

This was followed by their level of satisfaction with regards to the regularity of the street lights being put on and also maintenance issues.

Out of the 100 respondents, 88 of them responded to this question. The field data gives the distribution of their responses and indicated that majority of the respondents constituting 60% indicating that they are satisfied and 28% indicating that they are not satisfied with the street lights.

4.3.5 Source of drinking water

The well-being of household members to a very large extent is dependent on the availability of and accessibility to safe drinking water. Sources of drinking water can have tremendous effects on disease burdens of households. For example, clean drinking water can help to reduce water-borne diseases such as diarrhoea, bilharzia, typhoid and cholera. This can help to promote a healthy and productive life.

The sources of water can be classified as 'improved' or 'unimproved' sources. Safe water sources include piped public water into homes, public stand pipes, protected (lined) dug wells, boreholes and protected collected rain water. The unimproved sources are wells that are unprotected, vendors and tanker-trucks (WHO and UNICEF, 2000, cited in GSS, 2013, p. 393).

Out of the 100 respondents, 94 of them responded to this question. The proportion of respondents who indicated that they have potable water in their homes constitutes 62%, with 32% responding that they do not have potable water in their homes.

Similarly, on the question of what is their main source of water supply. From the data, there are six main sources of water supply for the households as follows: inside pipe stand, which constituted 50%; pipe in neighbouring house, which constituted 21%; water vending/tanker services, which constituted 3%; bore holes, which constituted 18%; wells, which constituted 7%; and rainwater, which constituted 1%.

4.3.6 Source of energy for cooking

Another indicator that can be used to measure the standard of living and human development of a household is the source of energy for cooking.

There were four non-respondents to this question. The main sources of cooking are charcoal, firewood, liquefied petroleum gas and electricity. The study revealed that majority of the respondents, 76%, use liquefied petroleum gas followed by households that use charcoal, constituting 19%, with 1% using electricity.

4.3.7 Sanitation: toilet facilities

One of the important indicators of a sanitary condition is a hygienic and efficient disposal method of human waste. Public health is one of the indirect ways of measuring a household's socio-economic status. However, it is often a neglected aspect of development in global South countries. The field data gives the distribution of toilet facilities in the households selected for the study. Out of the 100 respondents, three did not respond to this question.

There are five main sources of toilet facilities in Ghana. The highest facilities reported are: in-house flush toilet also known as water closet (WC) constituting 46% of the responses; in-house pit latrine constituting 21%; in-house Kumasi ventilated improved pit (KVIP) constituting 2% of the responses; public toilet (flush/KVIP/WC) constituting 25% of the responses; toilet in another house constituting 1% of the responses; households with no toilet facilities constituting 3%.

4.3.8 Sanitation: disposal of refuse (solid waste)

Adopting a modern and hygienic system of solid waste disposal in both rural and urban areas of Ghana has been a major challenge. An acceptable and hygienic waste management system helps to prevent the breed and spread of some contagious diseases and also helps to contribute to the improvement of the quality and sustainability of the environment. From the field data, the most commonly used medium of solid waste disposal is the public dump, which is dumping in either a container or an open dump site, constituting 49% of the responses. This is followed by the medium where the solid waste is collected for a fee, constituting 43% of the responses. Solid wastes that are burned by household constitute 6% of the responses, with 1% disposing their solid waste in other ways not indicated in any of the options provided.

4.4 Education and human capital

Education provides the vital tool for the general development of every society, hence it is a critical indicator for measuring human development. Accordingly, the GSS (2013) defines education as the process whereby people acquire knowledge, skills, attitudes and values to enable them to develop fully their human capital for the well-being of society.

Ordinarily, one could argue that there should be a positive relationship between the mining boom on one hand and development in education on the other hand. In like manner, the United Nation Development

Programme (UNDP, 2011) affirmed this notion when it reported that there is a correlation between education, human resource development and general economic growth.

Consequently, countries the world over, especially those in the developed North, place high emphasis on formulating and implementing educational policies that promote human development. Similarly, education is also seen as one of the components of human development that can help to eradicate the three ills of society, namely poverty, ignorance and disease. It is as a result of this that both the Millennium Development Goals (MDGs) and the Sustainable Development Goals (SDGs) have education as one of their development strategies. The importance of spending mineral rents on human skills development was acknowledged by a mineral resource academic expert interviewed as part of the studies, who responded that:

> The rents from the mining sector must be used to develop other sectors of the economy and more importantly, the human resources. Since mining is a capital-intensive sector, not many people can be employed in that sector; therefore, mineral rents should be spent in other sectors that can create jobs. Also it should be spent on the human skills development of the people.
>
> (Interview with a mineral resource expert, University of Ghana, 30 July 2017)

Although Ghana has made high gains in achieving the universal basic education as a result of the introduction of the Free Compulsory Universal Basic Education (FCUBE) policy, which was adopted by the government in 1961, there still remain huge challenges in quality education especially at the basic level, as well as affordability challenges in the second and tertiary levels of education (GSS, 2013).

4.4.1 Access to education in the Western Region

4.4.1.1 Construction of schools

The respondents from the Western Region of Ghana, where mining is done on a large scale, were asked to respond to the question of whether mining revenues have contributed to the construction of schools in their communities. The field data indicates that 99 out 100 responded to this question. From their responses, a vast majority of the respondents, constituting 85%, indicated in the affirmative, with 14% disagreeing with the question.

When they were asked for further explanations to justify their responses, some of those who responded in the affirmative added that the mining companies only construct schools in their catchment areas. Others also explained that apart from the schools, the mining companies also provide school buses, community centres and the establishment of scholarships for but brilliant but needy students.

Similarly, the respondents were asked to indicate the number of schools in their communities. The field data gives the distribution of their responses, which may only reflect the situation in their local and immediate communities.

The field data shows that 39% of the responses indicated that there are six to ten schools in their communities. The respondents who opted for one to five constitutes 9%, 11 to 15 represents 6% of the respondents, 15 and above represents 3%, other responses not indicated represents 1%. Also 26% of the respondents were unaware of the number of schools in their communities and 16% did not indicate any of the options given. The field data therefore supports that the mining companies fund the construction of schools in especially mining communities. In order to compare this with secondary data from the District and Municipal Education offices of the three districts selected for the study, efforts were made to obtain such data, however only one, Tarkwa Nsuaem municipality provided such data. In the 2010 census, the GSS (2013) estimated the population of Tarkwa Nsuaem at 90,477. The average annual population growth has been 2.5%, which means that from 2010 to 2015, the municipality's population has grown to about 101,786. It is estimated that those aged 0–24 years old constitute 58.3% of the total population. As a result, the estimated number of people from kindergarten to senior high school is 59,342 people.

4.4.1.2   *Types of schools in the community*

Ghana's educational system can be categorised into the basic level, second cycle level and the tertiary level. The field data gives the various types of educational institutions in the country. These are nursery/day care/primary schools, junior secondary/technical/vocational schools, tertiary institutions/universities/polytechnics/training colleges.

A vast majority of the respondents representing 80% indicated that all the above-mentioned types of schools exist in their communities. Respondents who indicated that only nursery/day care/primary schools exist in their community constituted 5%, 7% indicated that there are only junior secondary schools, 2% indicated only senior secondary/technical vocational schools, 3% indicated only tertiary institutions/universities/

polytechnics/training colleges and 3% did not respond to any of the options given. The available data shows that all types of schools exist in the Western Region. On the other hand, secondary data obtained from the Tarkwa Nsuaem municipality revealed a rather pyramid nature of the number of schools in the municipality and the entire Western Region. From the field data, the municipality has 67 kindergartens, 68 primary schools, 56 junior high schools, three senior high schools and one tertiary institution. There are more schools at the basic education levels with very few schools at the second cycle and tertiary levels. This trend, however, is not different from what exists in other non-mining regions of Ghana. This is because most education policy interventions in the past have focused on increasing access to the basic education to the neglect of the tertiary level.

4.4.1.3 Sources of funding schools in the community

Funding plays a critical role in the access, affordability and overall quality of education. The sources of funding for schools can vary depending on the ownership of the school and the purpose of its establishment, among other factors. The one who funds these educational institutions has a key stake in its running.

In Ghana, the sources of funding include public sources (government), private individuals, mining companies (in the case of mining communities) and non-governmental organisations (NGOs). The field data gives the distribution of the various sources of funding for the schools in the mining communities. Out of the 100 respondents, 96 of them responded to this question.

The field data gives a narrow majority of the respondents constituting 54% indicating that schools in their communities are funded by all four above-mentioned sources. The proportion of respondents who indicated that the sources of funding for schools come from public (government) only constituted 18%, 13% indicated private individuals only, 7% indicated the mining companies only, 5% NGOs only.

4.4.1.4 School enrolment in the Western Region

Basic education in Ghana generally consists of two years of kindergarten, six years of primary school and three years of junior high school. In each of the levels of education, respondents were asked to indicate the enrolment of students by ranking on the scale of very high, high, low and very low. The field data shows the distribution of their responses. Out of the 100 responses, 98 responded to this question.

The field data shows that a vast majority of the respondents constituting 83% indicated that enrolment at the basic level is high, 12% indicated that enrolment at this level is very high, 2% indicated that enrolment at this level is low and 1% indicated that enrolment is very low at this level. Generally, enrolment is high at the basic level of education.

Similarly, respondents were made to rank the enrolment at the second cycle level (which includes senior secondary school, technical schools and vocational schools). The secondary school level is made up of four years of schooling. The field data shows the distribution of the responses of the selected heads of households. Out of the 100 respondents, 97 responded to this question.

The field data shows that 79% of the respondents, representing a majority, opined that enrolment at the second cycle level is high, 11% indicated that enrolment at this level is very high, 7% indicated that the enrolment is low with nobody indicating that it is very low. Secondary data obtained from Tarkwa Nsuaem, however, reveals that for a population of 59,341 being between 0–24 years, there are three secondary schools with no vocational or technical school in the municipality. Critics have, however, argued that this is not different from other parts of Ghana, and can be explained as a legacy of the colonial educational system.

On the enrolment at the tertiary level (which includes universities, polytechnics, teacher training colleges, nursing and health colleges), the field data shows that a majority of the respondents, constituting 74%, stated that enrolment at the tertiary level is high, 5% indicated that enrolment at this level is very high, 18% indicated that it's low but nobody opined that it is very low. The Western Region can boast of few tertiary institutions since nationally there are not many institutions in relation to the population. However, unlike the basic and secondary education, many students travel outside their towns and home regions to access tertiary education especially in Accra, Kumasi and Cape Coast, which have the nation's prestigious tertiary institutions. Furthermore, one other reason that could account for the high rate of tertiary education despite the very low number of institutions could be the introduction of the distance learning, sandwich (summer schools) and evening programmes, which help to increase access at this level.

4.4.2 Affordability of education in the Western Region

Affordability of education is a key determinant of development in the educational sector and other factors, such as access and quality education, are closely related to education. In order to ascertain whether the respondents are able to afford the cost of education, they were first asked to indicate if there were children of school-going age in their household. The field data gives a distribution of their responses and indicates that 96 out the 100 respondents responded to this question. The data shows that a majority of the respondents, constituting 84%, said that they have children of school-going age in their household, whereas 12% responded in the negative. Affordable education at the basic level in Ghana generally has been boosted by the introduction of the Free Compulsory Basic Education policy. This policy initiated by the government of Ghana has not only made education at the basic level affordable but also compulsory. The school feeding programme, also introduced by the government, which ensures that children at the basic level are fed in school for free, has equally contributed to this response.

The respondents were also asked to indicate whether their children of school-going age are in school. The field data gives that 16 out of the 100 respondents did not respond to this question. The proportion of respondents who stated affirmatively constitutes 77% with 7% responding negatively that their children of school-going age in their households were not in school.

Consequently, the field data shows the distribution of whether the respondents can afford their children's school fees. Out of the 100 respondents, 19 of them did not respond to this question. The field data shows that majority, constituting 77%, of the heads of households indicated that they are able to afford the cost of school fees for the children of school-going age in their household. A very small minority of 4%, however, responded that they are not able to afford the cost of the school fees of the children.

Similarly, the heads of the households were also asked to indicate their opinion about whether they think other parents, who may be their friends, family members, church members or even neighbours, are able to afford the cost of their ward's school fees. The field data indicates that 89 out 100 of the respondents responded to this question. A majority of 77% responded that other parents are able to afford the cost of their school fees, while 14% responded in the negative.

When asked for their explanations to buttress their responses on how affordable they think school fees are, some of those who responded in the affirmative noted that, although the school fees is expensive, they are willing to make sacrifices in order to pay. Others opined that most parents who are gainfully employed are able to afford very good schools for the children in their households. As a coping strategy, some of the respondents, among those who are able to afford the cost of the school fees, revealed that they had secured loans to enable them pay for the fees. On the other hand, some of the respondents who said that they are not able to afford the cost of the school fees for their children indicated that the school fees are very expensive whereas others also explained that the cost of living is very high coupled with high unemployment in their communities. Secondary data from the district education office indicates that, for example, in Tarkwa Nsuaem municipality, for children between 0 and 24 years old, out of 59,341 of them, 33,240 are in school. This means that about 26,101 children of school-going age in that municipality alone are out of school from kindergarten to senior high school.

4.4.3 *Quality of education in the Western Region*

The quality of education determines the calibre of students that will be produced and is one of the relevant variables in education alongside accessibility and affordability of education.

Accordingly, the study asked the respondents to indicate whether there are enough trained teachers in their communities. This is because these parents attend parent–teacher association meetings of their wards where these issues are discussed. Of the 100 respondents, 96 indicated their responses to this question.

The field data shows that a vast majority of 90% of the respondents indicated that there are many trained teachers in the various schools in their communities. The remaining respondents responded in the negative. Secondary data obtained from district education office shows that there are 885 trained teachers in the Tarkwa Nsuaem district for 194 public institutions, whereas the private institutions have 86 trained teachers for 150 schools.

Similarly, the field data gives the proportion of the ratio of trained teachers to the number of children in the community. Out of the 100 respondents, six did not respond to this question.

The field data shows that 72% of the respondents indicated that there are many teachers in relation to the number of children in the various schools in their communities. A minority of the respondents who responded in the negative constitute 22%. In their explanations, some of those who responded in the negative said that most of the qualified teachers prefer to live in cities and refuse postings to the rural parts of their communities. As a result, there were others who explained that the teacher–pupil ratio in their communities is high. They also expressed that some of the schools in the mining communities still lack trained teachers. Secondary data collected from the Tarkwa Nsuaem municipality shows that there are 53,310 students at the basic level, with

971 trained teachers. The ratio is therefore one trained teacher to 55 students. This is more than twice the national average of one trained teacher is to 25 students.

The performance of students at the Basic Education Certificate Examination (BECE) and the Senior High School Certificate Examination are also important indicators to measure the quality of education in the Western Region and Ghana as a whole.

In view of this, the respondents were asked to rate the general performance of students in the BECE. The study categorised the rating into excellent, very good, good, poor and very poor. The field data gives the distribution of their ratings and shows that 97 out of the 100 respondents responded to this question.

The majority of the respondents, constituting 63%, indicated that the performance of the pupils has been good, 30% indicated that performance has been very good, 2% rated that the performance has been excellent. The proportion of respondents who rated that the performances of the pupils have been poor constitutes 2% with nobody indicating that the performance have been very poor. According to secondary data from the Tarkwa Nsuaem municipal education office, out of 2,755 pupils who sat for the BECE, 2,314 passed (84%). Similarly, at the West African Senior School Certificate Examination, out of the 901 students who sat for the examination, 897 (99.5%) passed. This means that performance at the basic and second cycle level is very high compared with other parts of Ghana.

Furthermore, quality education does not exclude technical and vocational education. As a result of this, the respondents were asked whether there are vocational and technical institutions in their area.

The field data shows show that the majority of the heads of the households, constituting 71%, indicated that there are technical and vocational institutions as well as training centres in their communities. A minority of 24% indicated that there are no such institutions in their communities.

Ideally, revenues from mining should contribute to education in general. As a result, the study wanted to find out if mining has contributed to literacy in the Western Region. Literacy has to do with the ability to read and write. The field data gives the proportion of the respondents' responses on whether mining has contributed to literacy in the region.

Of the 100 responders, 17 of them did not respond to this question. From their responses, the majority of the respondents, constituting 66%, indicated that mining has contributed to the literacy rate in the Western Region. The proportion of respondents who expressed that the mining sector has not contributed to the literacy rate in their communities constitutes 17%. In explaining their reasons, some of those who expressed that the mining sector mining has contributed to the literacy rate said that the mining companies have supported the construction of schools in the communities. Other respondents further explained that some mining companies operating in the region have introduced scholarship schemes for brilliant but needy students in the community. On the contrary, some of those who expressed that the mining sector has not contributed to literacy rate in the community gave the following reasons. First, some said that many of the youth in the community drop out of school to engage in small-scale mining (mainly illegal mining, popularly known in Ghana as "galamsey"). Second, some bemoaned the inadequate school infrastructures, facilities and other teaching and learning materials in the various schools in their communities, and added that the general support that the schools used to get from the mining companies has drastically dwindled. Third, others were of the opinion that the mining companies do not have literacy programmes for the communities.

4.5 Medical care in the Western Region

Medical care and the general health of a people is one of the most crucial determinants of human development of any society. As a result, development that is people-centred must also be concerned with factors such as accessible, affordable and quality healthcare.

These various factors correlate with vital health statistical indicators such as life expectancy rate, maternal mortality rate, infant mortality rate and the general health of a population.

In Ghana, the introduction of the National Health Insurance Scheme (NHIS) in 2003 marked a major turning point in healthcare delivery in the country, especially in terms of access and affordability of basic healthcare delivery. That notwithstanding, healthcare delivery still remains a major challenge in many parts of the country. It is in view of this that the study sought to find out the state of healthcare delivery in the Western mineral wealth region of Ghana to ascertain whether mineral revenues are being invested in the health sector of the region.

4.5.1 Access to medical care in the Western Region

One major reform that has taken place in Ghana's health sector has been the introduction of the NHIS. It was introduced by the government of Ghana to address the problem of financial barrier to healthcare posed by the 'cash and carry system' of healthcare, which required out-of- pocket payment for healthcare at the point of service delivery.

In trying to investigate the accessible nature of healthcare in the Western Region, the study asked the respondents to indicate the number of hospitals in their communities. From the field data, 99 out of the 100 respondents responded to this question. The number of hospitals were categorised in the range of 1–5, 6–10, 11–15, other and unaware. The field data indicates that a narrow majority of the respondents, constituting 53%, stated that there are 6–10 hospitals in their communities, 22% indicated 1–5 hospitals, 5% indicated 11–15 hospitals, 1% of the respondents indicated a number of hospitals not captured in the options and 18% indicated that they are not aware of the number of hospitals in their communities. The responses clearly indicate that there are a number of both public and private health facilities in the Western Region. Table 4.1 shows the number of health facilities in the Tarkwa Nsuaem municipality with a population of 90,477 (GSS, 2013).

The heads of households were also asked to indicate the different types of health facilities in their communities. The types of health facilities in Ghana are community-based health planning services (CHPS), clinics, polyclinics and hospitals. Respondents were also given the option 'not aware'. The field data indicates that Tarkwa Nsuaem municipality has, for example, all the different types of health facilities in the country.

The field data indicates that 33% of the respondents indicated that they have all the different types of health facilities in their communities. Whereas 20% of the respondents indicated clinics only, 7% indicated CHPS only, 33% of the respondents indicated hospitals only, 1% indicated polyclinics only and 6% of the respondents indicated that they are not aware of the types of health facilities in their communities.

Table 4.1 Health facilities in Tarkwa Nsuaem municipality

Health facilities	Public	Private	Total
Hospitals	2	5	7
Health centres	5	0	5
Clinics	3	8	11
Reproductive and child health (RCH) centres	2	0	2
Maternity homes	0	2	2
Community-based health planning services (CHPS)	14	0	14
Total	**26**	**15**	**41**

Source: Field data Municipal Health Directorate, Tarkwa Nsuaem, 2016.

On the subject of ownership of the health facilities, who are also the service providers, the respondents were asked to indicate the owners and financiers of the various health facilities. The field data indicates the distribution of the various categories of ownership, namely, government, private individuals, the community and mining companies.

The field data indicates a narrow majority of 58% of the respondents suggested that all the various forms of ownership are found in their communities, with 18% of the respondents indicating government, 13% indicating private individuals, 1% indicating the community and 7% indicating the mining companies. The number of respondents who responded to other ownership forms that were not captured by the options given constitutes 2%. The field data and shows that there are two main types of ownership in the Tarkwa Nsuaem municipality: public and private ownership. The public ownership is mainly by the government of Ghana whereas the private ownership is either private individuals, mining companies and faith-based organisations.

In addition to this, the study wanted to find out if the mining companies operating in the Western Region have instituted a health insurance scheme for the people in the communities they are operating in. The field data indicates the health insurance of the households and shows that out of the 100 respondents, 92 of them responded to this question.

The field data indicates that 67% of the respondents responded that there is no such health insurance scheme in the Western Region apart from the National Health Insurance Scheme introduced by the state.

The proportion of responses who indicated in the affirmative constitutes 25%. In explaining their stance, some of those who responded in the affirmative indicated that most of the mining companies have their own insurance policies for their workers but not for the entire community.

Again, the respondents were asked to rate the overall access to health facilities in their communities and the Western Region as a whole. The field data indicates that 98 out of the 100 respondents responded to this question.

The field data shows the rating on the range of very high, high, low and very low. A vast majority of 90% of the respondents indicated that people's access to health facilities and healthcare is high. Those who indicated that it is very high constituted 4%. 2% responded low with the remaining 2% also responding very low. In explaining their points, those who responded in the affirmative noted that, first, there were several health centres in their communities, hence the high access to healthcare. Second, the introduction of the NHIS, which is also accepted by most of the health centres and facilities, both private and public, has equally increased the accessibility of healthcare in the Western Region. On the contrary, however, some of the respondents who responded in the negative explained that the health facilities in their communities are inadequate.

4.5.2 Affordable medical care

Affordable healthcare was one of the main reasons for the introduction of the NHIS. Prior to the introduction of the scheme, the general cost of healthcare was expensive especially for the average Ghanaian. The respondents of the study were asked to indicate whether the cost of healthcare is affordable. The field data shows the distribution of the respondents' responses on whether the cost of healthcare is affordable. The data shows that out of the 100 responses, 97 of them responded to this question.

From the field data, a majority of 74% of the respondents indicated that they are able to afford the cost of healthcare in their communities. The proportion of respondents who are not able to afford the cost of healthcare for themselves and other members of the household constituted 23%. In explaining their points, those who responded in the affirmative noted that, first, they utilise the NHIS and that it is expensive to pay for healthcare without it, and as a result most of them access this insurance scheme. On the contrary, those who responded negatively explained that they are unable to afford the cost of healthcare because the NHIS is not working effectively and that it does not cover all ailments. This according to them is gradually ushering them back to the days of the 'cash and carry' era, the system where a patient has to pay in cash before they can access healthcare in the various health facilities.

4.5.3 Quality of healthcare in the Western Region

Quality healthcare is essential for the health needs of every society and should therefore be given the attention it deserves. The respondents were asked questions with the view to measuring the quality of healthcare in the Western Region. The respondents were asked to estimate the mortality rate among children below five years in their communities. The field data shows the distribution of the respondents' perspective of the mortality rate of children below five years. The respondents were to rate their responses on the categories of very high, high, low and very low. Out of the 100 respondents, 98 of them responded to this question. A vast majority of the respondents constituting 79% indicated that infant mortality rate is low in their communities. However, 14% indicated that the infant mortality rate in their communities is high, with 5% indicating that it is very low. The percentage of respondents who did not answer to this question constitute 2%.

However, secondary data from the district health directorate of the Takwa Nsuaem municipality indicates that infant mortality rate in 2015 was 12.3. This is lower than Ghana's national infant mortality rate of 41 recorded between 2010 and 2014 (GSS, 2015).

Furthermore, the respondents were asked to indicate whether there are enough trained doctors and nurses in the various health facilities available in their communities. The field data gives a proportion of their responses and indicate that out of the 100 respondents, 97 of them responded to this question. The field data indicates a majority of 80% were of the opinion that there are enough trained doctors and nurses in their communities, with 18% disagreeing.

The respondents were also asked to indicate whether the trained doctors and nurses were adequate in the various health facilities. The field data shows the proportion of their responses and indicate that out of the 100 respondents, 98 responded to this question. The proportion of respondents who responded in the affirmative is 69%, with 29% of the respondents responding in the negative.

Those who disagreed with the question explained that the doctor/nurse to patient ratio is very high because most of the doctors especially refuse postings to the remote parts of their communities. Secondary data from the district health directorate of Tarkwa Nsuaem indicates that with a population of 90,477 (GSS, 2013) and 41 different health facilities, there are nine medically trained doctors and 359 nurses in all categories. Consequently, the doctor–patient ratio in the second biggest municipality Tarkwa Nsuaem, selected for this study is 1:10,053, which is lower than Ghana's doctor–patient ratio of 1:10,170 but higher than the World Health Organization (WHO) recommendation, which is 1:6,000. The nurse–patient ratio in the municipality is 1:252 which is rather an improvement on the national nurse–patient ratio average of 1:24,533 (GSS, 2015).

In trying to investigate the role of the mining companies in the health sector of the Western Region, the respondents were asked if the mining companies are contributing to improved healthcare in their communities. The field data gives a proportion of their responses and shows that 88 responded to this question, out of 100. The field data indicates that 77% of the respondents were of the opinion that the mining companies are contributing to healthcare in the communities, such as by donating health equipment to the health facilities and helping to expand health facilities. The remaining 11% responded negatively.

Those who responded in the affirmative explained that, first, some of the mining companies have constructed hospitals that are opened to the general public. Second, some of the mining companies have also provided health facilities and infrastructure to the community. Third, some further added that the mining companies have inadequate health facilities to cater for the health needs of their workers, or sometimes pay the health expenses for their workers. Nevertheless, while the field data confirms that mining companies contribute to healthcare, the International Council on Mining and Metals (2015) reports in a study of mining in Ghana that 66% of its respondents identified one of the negative effects of mining as health problems. This means that the contribution of mining to healthcare can both be positive and negative.

4.6 Opportunities for jobs and skilled labour force

Ordinarily, mining activities should create jobs for people in the communities in which it takes place. Nevertheless, mining is a capital-intensive sector and therefore cannot create more direct human jobs for people, but rather its existence, operations and revenues can create indirect job opportunities. As a result of this, the study has as part of its objectives to investigate how mining can create sustainable jobs to improve the livelihoods of the people in the Western Region. In order to achieve this objective, the study first asked the respondents to indicate the main occupation of the people in the Western Region.

The field data shows the distribution of the various occupations of the respondents and shows that the main occupations in the community are categorised into farming, trading, fishing and mining. The field data shows that 41% of the respondents indicated that their main occupation is mining, 39% said trading, 19% said farming, 1% said fishing.

Similarly, this discussion is useful in the context of Africa's lack of diversified economies. As a result, the respondents were asked to indicate whether they agree that the mining sector in the community has attracted more of people's attention and investment to the detriment of other occupations in the community. The field data shows the distribution of their responses in this regard and indicate that 97 out of the 100 respondents responded to this question, with 81% agreeing to the assertion that the mining sector has created a mono-economy in the mining communities. The remaining 16% of the respondents disagreed with the assertion. Those who responded in the affirmative explained that mining has taken over their farmlands. They say that this is negatively affecting the agricultural sector in their communities. Other respondents further added that the mining activities have polluted their farmlands, making agricultural activities in mining towns and communities very close to the mining sites virtually impossible.

This findings contradict a response from the official of the Ghana Chamber of Mines who responded to the question of whether they agree that mining has clouded other sectors such as agriculture in especially mining communities:

> Not necessarily. The issue of job sustainability is very critical. The critical question is how we can channel mining resources into other sectors such as such as manufacturing and agriculture to create sustainable jobs. In view of this, every mining company has introduced the 'alternative livelihood programme', for example Tarkwa goldfields is into oil palm plantation.
>
> (Interview with the public relations officer of the
> Ghana Chamber of Mines, 10 July 2016)

Some respondents further explained that 'everyone' wants to work in the mines to the extent that most of the youth who are not employed in the mining companies are into illegal mining locally known as '*galamsey*'. On the contrary, those who responded negatively to the assertion explained that the trading sector in particular has seen a boost, since some of the people employed in the mining sector spend part of their income in the community and this has led to the creation of jobs in this area for many of the local people.

Equally important is the issue of unemployment. As such, the respondents were asked to rate the unemployment situation in their communities. The field data shows the proportion of their responses rating unemployment on a scale of very high, high, low and very low. The distribution shows that 59% of the respondents rated unemployment as high, 29% as very high and 12% as low. None of the respondents rated unemployment as very low in their communities. This means that an overwhelming 88% of the heads of the households rated unemployment as either high or very high.

Besides unemployment, the categories of available jobs were also of interest to the study. The respondents were asked to indicate whether mining in the community has contributed to the employment of some community members in highly skilled jobs in the mining companies. The field data indicates the distribution of their responses and indicates that 95 out of the 100 respondents responded to this question.

The field data indicates that 73% of the respondents indicated that mining has contributed to highly skilled jobs in the community, while

22% indicated in the negative. To buttress their positions, those who responded in the affirmative said that only members in the communities with skilled manpower are employed. Others also explained that only few of the educated and skilled people are employed and that even currently the mining companies are embarking on a retrenchment exercise. There was also the explanation that sometimes the unskilled people are employed and trained, whereas for others, the mining companies apply a local content policy. Some also added that employment was based on skills specialisation. On the contrary, those who responded negatively also explained that they didn't see the importance of mining because most of the youth in their communities and the Western Region as a whole are unemployed.

Similarly, the respondents were asked to indicate whether mining in their communities has contributed to the employment of unskilled labour-intensive jobs in and outside the mining companies. The field data shows the proportion of their responses and indicates that 94 out of the 100 respondents responded to this question, with 63% stating that mining has contributed to the employment of unskilled labour intensive jobs in their communities. A minority of the respondents, constituting 31%, responded in the negative.

In explaining their points, those who responded in the affirmative said that a few unskilled people are employed in mainly subcontracted mining jobs. With such few job opportunities, they sometimes have to pay bribes before they are employed. Others also added that some of the unskilled are also employed in both small-scale legal mining and small-scale illegal mining. On the contrary, those who responded negatively also explained that the youth in the communities are unskilled and so do not get jobs in the mining sector. While others further explained that there are no unskilled jobs unless one pays a bribe.

Equally important to the study is the structural dependency theory which explains that the extraction of raw materials by Western countries in their former colonies is detrimental to the development of the local people in these countries (Frank, 1967). As a result, the study asked the respondents to rate the extent to which they feel that the mining companies in their communities make a lot of profit while the community remains poor. The field data shows the proportion of the ratings and indicates that 99 out of the 100 respondents responded to this question. From the field data, the range for the rating are strongly agree, agree, disagree and strongly disagree. The responses show that 63% rated that they agree with the assertion while 26% rated that they strongly agree. A small minority of the respondents representing 10% indicated that they disagree with the assertion. This therefore means that a majority of 89% of the respondents either agree or strongly agree that the mining companies in their communities make a lot of profit while the local communities remain poor.

To explain their stance, those who responded in the affirmative said that the mining companies are siphoning the resources from the communities without any benefit to the communities. Others added that the community is still poor because there are no jobs. For others, the reason is that there are still poor social amenities and infrastructural facilities despite the mining activities in their communities, while some of the respondents explained that mining has taken over their farmlands and displaced many people from their homes and livelihoods and that in most cases the land acquisition compensation is very low. On the contrary, however, some of the respondents who disagreed with this assertion explained that mining has contributed to general development in the community and they cite the educational sector in particular as having benefited from the contributions from the mining sector. Consequently, the World Bank (2014) in its internal evaluation report noted that the government of Ghana's effort to utilise the country's mineral revenues to promote people-centred development was still a work in progress.

Along with this, the respondents were also asked if their communities would be better off without the mining operations. The field data indicates the distribution of their responses and indicates that 95 out of the 100 heads of households responded to this question. From their responses, a narrow majority of 59% responded that their community would not be better off without mining in their communities, while 36% responded that their communities would be better off without mining.

In explaining their positions, the respondents who responded against mining said that, first, if there was no mining in their communities, agriculture, especially farming, will have be done on a large scale because many people would be attracted into it. Second, only few people are benefiting either directly as in the case of employment, or indirectly as in the case of enjoying the social interventions and social infrastructures funded from the royalties and revenues of mining. Besides this, mining is destroying their environment and that their community is worse off in terms of general development compared with other non-mining communities in Ghana. The field data confirms a study by the International Council on Mining and Metals (2015) that reports that the negative effects of mining in Ghana include destruction of the environment, collapse of livelihoods, health problems and social vices. This means that whereas a majority of the respondents on one hand agree that the mining companies make a lot of profit to the detriment of the development of the Western Region in general, at the same time most of them were also of the opinion that their communities would have been worse off without the mining activities. Those who responded in this way also said that, first, there is huge potential in mining, however this potential can only be fully realised if mining is responsibly managed to create jobs and diversify economic activities. Second, others added that they were of the opinion that mining operations in the community has resulted in the booming of the sales and trading sector in the area.

On the issue of how mining can be done responsibly to promote social development, the respondents were asked to indicate what can be done to ensure that mining communities benefit from the mineral wealth of their land. The field data indicates that 98 out of the 100 respondents responded to this question. From their responses, the respondents were given the options of establishing a mining community development fund, enacting mineral revenue management laws, moving towards state ownership of mining companies and also to express other opinions that may not have been captured.

The field data indicates that a 51% majority of the respondents opted for the establishment of a mining community development fund, 36% for laws to be enacted to regulate the management and use of mineral revenues and 7% supported moving towards state ownership of mining companies. Ghana currently has a Minerals Development Fund, however authors such as Standing (2014), Pedro (2005), Pegg, (2006) and Allen and Thomas, (2000) have argued that the main problems with the Fund have been the lack of clear legislative policy on how it should be spent, the lack of transparency and accountability as well as participation in the mineral governance structure of Ghana.

4.7 Transparency and accountability

Transparency and accountability are two buzzwords in development management and studies. The two concepts are closely related and involve accessible information, institutions and processes. Transparency and accountability are pivotal to the governance concept and the definition and measurement of development in general. From this understanding, the discussion explored the extent to which the current governance system is transparent and promotes accountability with the aim of promoting people-centred development.

The respondents' knowledge of the mineral resources in their community was tested. They were specifically asked to indicate if their communities are rich in mineral resources. The field data gives a distribution of their responses and indicates that 97 out of the 100 respondents responded to this question. The field data shows that a very vast majority of 95% of the respondents indicated that they are aware that their communities are rich in mineral resources with 2% responding in the negative.

The respondents were asked to indicate the main mineral resources extracted from their locality. The field data gives the distribution of their responses and indicates that out of the 100 respondents, three of them did not respond to this question. The main mineral resources in Ghana are gold, diamond, bauxite, manganese and other minerals in smaller quantities. The field data indicates that the proportion of respondents who responded that their communities have all the minerals listed constitutes a narrow majority of 58%, with 19% indicating gold, 5% diamond, 3% bauxite, 13% manganese and 1% indicated other minerals not mentioned in the options given.

Furthermore, the respondents were asked to express their opinion on whether mineral resources have a role to play in the development of their communities and Ghana as a whole. The field data gives the distribution of their responses and indicates that almost all the respondents, constituting 97%, opined that mineral resources have a role to play in national development. Only 3% of the respondents answered in the negative.

In explaining their various positions, some of those who responded in the affirmative gave various reasons to substantiate their claims. To some, the country generates revenues from mineral resources through taxes and royalties, and when these revenues are used responsibly it can promote socio-economic development. Others explained that mining can promote investments and employment in the country while some also added that royalties from the mining companies to the communities can be used to promote development interventions for the benefit of the people in the communities. Besides this, some explained that the mining activities have helped to boost trading activities in most of the mining towns. While some of the respondents agree that mining can promote socio-economic development, they however added that this can happen under a condition. To them, there is the need for incorruptible people to be elected into leadership positions since corruption is a major hindrance to revenues and royalties from minerals being used for people-centred development interventions. Other respondents indicated the need for funds from minerals to be used judiciously in priority areas for the general good of the people in Ghana. On the contrary, the few who responded in the negative also explained that, first, the cost of living has been very high even in the mining communities and, second, that mining causes severe environmental damage to their communities.

At the community and national level, respondents were asked whether they or other members of their households benefit from the mining sector. The field data gives the proportion of their responses and indicates that a majority of 85% of the respondents indicated that neither they nor other members of their household benefit either directly or indirectly from the mining revenues and royalties, while a minority of 14% indicated that either they or other members of their households have benefited directly or indirectly from the mining sector.

Some of the explanations from those who responded that they had not benefited are that only the chiefs and those closely related to the royal stools benefit from the royalties and other opportunities related to the mining sector. This situation is due to the lack of transparency and accountability in the access and utilisation of the royalties and mineral revenues. Others maintained that the cost of living is very high and that the mining sector has not helped them in any way, adding that only those who work directly with the mining companies and their related sectors benefit from the wealth of the minerals. Irresponsible use of the mineral funds was also once again identified by the respondents as being a major reason why they think they don't benefit from the mining sector. They particularly did not understand why the colossal amount of money from the mining sector has not been used to fund socio-economic development in their communities. The field data and particularly this assertion is similar to the study findings arrived at by WACAM, an NGO working in mining communities across Ghana, that 'mining communities surveyed perceive mining as not being beneficial to them'. Contrary to this, in an interview with the Minerals Commission of Ghana to find out if they agree that mineral resource rents have not benefited Ghanaians, the official of the Commission responded that;

> No, I wouldn't say that. In 2012, it contributed to 27% of government revenues. With the coming in of oil, 2015, it contributed to 14% of government revenues. Now look at all the buildings and development going on in Accra, i.e., roads. The challenge has been that government haven't labelled and indicated which of the projects are funded from the mineral revenue; that is why we are advocating for the Mineral Revenue Management Act.
>
> (Interview with the manager of sectorial policy and planning, Minerals Commission of Ghana, 4 July 2016)

He further admitted that the district assemblies, who are the local government authorities, spend their share of mining revenues on things that do not directly benefit the people.

They normally refer to it at recurrent expenditure, and sometimes they use part of the money to collect waste. We therefore normally tell them that minerals are resources that deplete, therefore revenues from it that come to them should be used for sustainable projects such as schools, hospitals and other tangible things so that posterity can appreciate the contribution from mining. So that was a problem we encountered with the district assemblies, so now the Commission and the Ministry of Finance have given them guidelines for the utilisation of mineral revenues since last year [2015]. We have also been encouraging the district assemblies to have a dedicated account for the mineral revenues that come to them.

(Interview with the manager of sectorial policy and planning,
Minerals Commission of Ghana, 4 July 2016)

Similarly, previous financial audits in the district assemblies have brought to light serious financial irregularities including misappropriation of revenues and improper auditing systems, among others (EITI Report, 2016). Similarly, the IMF (2012, p. 101) had in its poverty reduction strategy confirmed that 'weak financial management practice is rampant and there is general lack of accountability and transparency in the utilization of the District Assemblies Common Fund and other resources at the district level'.

The issue of ownership of the mineral resources is equally important, as such, the respondents were asked to indicate who owns the minerals in the Western Region. The field data gives the distribution of the ownership of the mineral resources and shows that 97 out of the 100 respondents responded to this question. The possible owners that were provided are: the government of Ghana, the people in the community, the mining companies of Ghana and the traditional leaders in the mineral wealth communities.

The field data indicates that the majority of the respondents (64%) were of the opinion that the mineral deposits belong to the government of Ghana, 21% opted for mining companies, 11% opted for the traditional leaders and 1% opined that they belong to the people in the community. This means that the ownership of the minerals resources by the government of Ghana is widely acknowledged by most people.

Similarly, the control of mineral resources is also very important in its governance system. Consequently, the study asked the respondents to indicate who they think controls the minerals resources and the revenues from them. The field data gives the distribution of their responses and indicates that 97 out of the 100 respondents responded to this question.

The options given are government of Ghana, the people of Ghana, the minerals commission and the traditional leaders.

The field data indicates the distribution of their responses and indicates that 64% were of the opinion that the mineral resources are controlled by the government of Ghana, 21% opined that they are controlled by the mining companies, 11% indicated the traditional leaders and 1% indicated that it controlled by the people in the community.

The study further explored the management of the mineral resources. The respondents were asked who manages the mineral resources. The various options for the management of the resources are government of Ghana, the people of Ghana, mining companies, traditional leaders. The field data shows the distribution of their responses and indicates that 98 out of the 100 respondents responded to this question. The field data shows that the majority of the respondents (69%) responded that the government of Ghana manages the mineral resources and its revenues. Only 1% indicated that the community is in charge of the management, 22% indicated that the mining companies are in charge, with 6% opting for the traditional leaders.

In view of the data, the majority of Ghanaians are of the opinion that the mineral sector is managed by the government of Ghana.

The current mineral governance structure places the ownership, management and control of the mining sector on the central government. The study wanted to investigate whether the community can equally play a role in the ownership, control and management of the mineral resources. The field data shows the distribution of the respondents on their take on whether they think the community can play a role in the ownership, control and management of the mining sector. The field data indicates that 95 out of the 100 respondents responded to this question and shows that 66% of the respondents said that they don't think the community can play a role in the ownership, control and management of the mineral resources, with 29% responding that they believe it can.

The respondents gave varied views to substantiate their options. Some of those who responded in the affirmative responded that when the community is given the role to own, control and manage the mineral it will enhance participation and accountability and ensure that the people in the mining communities are actually part of the decision-making process. Others also added that if the community is given the responsibility to own, manage and control the resources, it will help to create jobs for most people in the community and help to redistribute wealth, which for them will bring sustainable development. On the contrary, those who responded in the negative felt that the community leaders (mainly the chiefs and other traditional leadership, the assembly men, the members and the district chief executives) are corrupt and will misappropriate the funds generated from the minerals. Some went a step further and claimed that the traditional leaders and the politicians are the same (they are all corrupt and dishonest). They explained that currently, the royalties that the chiefs and other traditional leaders receive are not spent in a transparent and accountable manner. Again, some explained that the community does not have the technical capacity to manage the mineral resources. A similar study by Standing (2014) revealed that too often, chiefs have tended not have an interest in investing mineral revenues in the development of their people. Besides, there are no transparency and accountability mechanisms on how the revenues are received and utilised. The lack of community stakeholder engagement and no proper regulation accounts for this (Boachie-Danquah, 2011).

Furthermore, explanations were offered that when the community is given the opportunity to own, control and manage the resources, the revenues and royalties will not be used to support sustainable development initiatives. In the same way, others were of the opinion that the revenues gotten from the mining sector should be used to subsidise the cost of basic social amenities such as water and electricity in the communities. For such people, such a move will ensure the equitable distribution of the mineral revenues.

The study also wanted to find out if the respondents would want to have a voice in the decision-making processes that leads to the selection of mining companies to operate in the communities. The field data gives the distribution of their responses and indicates that 48 of the respondents responded to this question. From data, 33% responded that indeed they would want to have a voice in the processes of mining company selection to the communities, while the remaining 15% responded in the negative.

There is therefore a general interest and willingness of communities to participate in mining-related decision-making to grant them the opportunity to express their views and concerns in the sector. This confirms an earlier work by Boachie-Danquah (2011) that there is a lack of community stakeholder engagement and no proper regulation that will ensure that people in communities can participate in mining-related decision-making.

In order to find out how transparent the current governance system is, the respondents were asked if they can easily access contractual agreements between the government of Ghana and the mining companies operating in their communities. The field data indicates the proportion of their responses and shows that two out of the 100 respondents did not respond to this question.

The field data shows that a vast majority of 95% responded that they can't access such information ,whereas 3% responded in the affirmative that they are able to access such information. However, in responding to the issue of whether local community people or their representatives are involved in the contractual process, the official of the Minerals Commission responded that:

> People have representatives in Parliament. I'm yet to see a country where the ordinary people are given copies of mining contract agreements. But as a standard practice, when the agreements are made by the attorney general and our legal team, then it goes through Parliament. The people's representative is in Parliament. So, for example, if there is something wrong [it will not benefit the people of Tarkwa] with an agreement between the government of Ghana and AngloGold Ashanti in Tarkwa, the Member of Parliament for Tarkwa is supposed to raise it for it to be addressed in Parliament.
>
> (Interview with the manager of sectorial policy and planning, Minerals Commission of Ghana, 4 July 2016)

Similarly, the respondents were asked if they can easily access information on payments made by mining companies to governments in the form of taxes and as well as the amounts of royalties that are go to the community leaders. The field data illustrates their responses and also shows an equally vast majority of the respondents (92%) indicated that they cannot access such information whereas 8% responded in the affirmative. Those who assented to the question explained that they are able to the access such information on the radio stations in the communities, local government leaders and those close to them, community non-governmental organisations whose focus is in the mining sector and the annual budget of the mining companies.

Furthermore, a specific question was asked as to whether the respondents know the amount of royalties and taxes paid by the mining companies to government of Ghana and whether these amounts are made public.

The field data indicates the proportion of their responses and illustrates that almost all the respondents (99%) responded that they don't know how much royalties the mining companies pay to the government, with only 1% saying that they did know. As a result of this there seems to be a limited information flow between the government, companies and the communities. However, when the question was posed to the official of the Ghana Chamber of Mines, an association of mining companies in Ghana, if they think Ghanaians know how much money the mining companies pay to the government in the form of corporate taxes and royalties, the official responded that;

> Yes, they do. For example, a billboard on the Tetteh Quashie round about that Newmont and Goldfields advertises how much they paid to government in 2015. They publish some in the daily papers. Not all the mining companies do that but Newmont and Goldfields especially do that. The two companies do that in their interest.
>
> The Chamber collates data of how much the mining companies paid to government in the form of corporate taxes annually. The data collected aggregates everything, all the taxes together so that for example AngloGold in Obuasi and Tarkwa, people in Obuasi wouldn't know how much exactly was paid in form of taxes.
>
> The EITI is a very good platform for transparency for which the Chamber is a founding member. Here each company reports how much corporate taxes, royalties and property taxes they pay to the government, local assemblies, and regulators. It is published in a report and distributed in the districts. The distribution is done through stakeholder fora where NGOs, civil society organizations are invited.
>
> (Interview with the public relations officer of
> Ghana Chamber of Mines, 10 July 2016)

Nevertheless, when the same question was posed to an official of WACAM, an NGO that advocates for the development of mining communities, the official responded that:

> The contract agreements that spell out the amount in terms of royalties that these companies pay to the government are not made public to the general public, not even the local mining communities.
> (Interview with the public relations officer of
> WACAM, 16 July 2017)

Narrowing it further, the respondents were asked their knowledge of the amount of monies the central government disburses to their local governments in the mining communities through their community heads. The field data indicates their proportion with regards to this and indicates that nearly all the respondents (99%) responded that they are not aware of the amount.

Equally important are groups, organisations or institutions that represent the interests of the communities in the process of contracting and disbursement of mineral revenues and how they are spent in the country as a whole and the Western Region specifically. In view of this, the heads of the household selected for this study were asked if there exist such groups or organisations and their knowledge of them. The field data indicates the proportion of their responses on their knowledge of civil society organisations that advocate for the development needs of the Western Region and show that 97 out of the 100 respondents expressed their opinion on this question.

The field data indicates that 87%, representing a majority of the respondents, were of the opinion that they are not aware of such groups and organisations, with 10% indicating that they are aware of such organisation or groups. Some of those responded in the affirmative identified some of the organisations as community radio stations, NGOs such as WACAM and some local community leaders.

Moreover, the respondents were asked to express their opinions about what they think can be done to ensure that government officials (who superintend over the mineral funds), mining companies and local community leaders who receive mineral royalties on behalf of the people utilise the funds in a transparent and accountable manner. From their responses, some suggested that, there should be a legislation to promote transparency and accountability or if such legislations exist already in the county's status books then there should be strict enforcement of such laws. Others were also of the opinion that corrupt officials should be prosecuted to serve as a deterrent while others called for honest leadership to control and manage the resources from minerals. Besides these, others opined that there should be encouragement of community participation and sensitisation backed by a legal framework. Others suggested that, instead of the current arrangements where the mining companies directly pay taxes and royalties to the government, rather the mining companies will do a better job if given the mandate to use the percentage due the community to directly develop the community. This to them will see a massive improvement in social interventions and infrastructural development. There was also the call for there to another regulatory body aside the Minerals Commission to have an oversight responsibility on the spending of mineral rents. This will ensure that mineral rents are used judiciously for socio-economic development of the country.

Unlike the respondents who were optimistic that there can be improvements provided the right things are done, there were others who were pessimistic and responded that the situation indeed looks hopeless to the extent that nothing can be done about it to bring improvement to especially mining communities and regions such as the Western Region of Ghana.

4.8 Equitable participation

Equitable participation has become one of the definitions of the concept of development. This is even more so since almost all known societies are made up of heterogeneous compositions. This means that society is made up of social differences and social stratification in terms of wealth, power, prestige and privileges (Nukunya, 2003). These social differences have led to unequal access to the various social goods and services in society. As a result of this, the study identified some of the social differences in the Ghanaian society to find out how the current governance structure in the mining sector positions them, in terms of access to job opportunities.

The issue of gender is one of such social differences; as such the respondents were asked whether the mining sector creates equal job opportunities for both males and females. The field data illustrates the distribution of the responses of the respondents and shows that out of the 100 respondents, 98 responded to this question. Their responses reveal that 54% indicated that the mining sector does not create equal opportunities for both males and females. The proportion of respondents who responded in the affirmative to this question constitutes 44%.

As a result, a slim majority of the people in the Western Region are of the opinion that the mining sector is gender biased in terms of opportunities for job creation. When asked for their explanation, some of those who responded in the affirmative explained that both males and females are working in the mines and that several of such women are in high positions. On the contrary, the majority who responded in the negative explained that work in the mines is very tedious and not for women, as a result only few females are employed in the administration.

Moreover, on the issue of the physically challenged persons and able-bodied people, the respondents were asked if the mining sector creates equal job opportunities for both physically challenged and able-bodied people. The field data indicates that 97 out of the 100 respondents responded to this question and that majority of the respondents (64%) indicated that currently the jobs available in the mining sector are biased towards able-bodied people to the detriment of persons with disabilities. The minority who thought this was not the case constitute 33% of the respondents. In the explanations of those who felt there was a bias toward the able-bodied, it was said that the nature of the jobs in the mines is not friendly to those who are physically challenged. The only time such people may be considered is when they get injured in the process of performing their duties – then they are taken care of and maintained in the mining companies.

On the issue of manual and mental labour, the respondents were asked to express their opinions on whether they think the mining sector creates equal job opportunities for both the literate and illiterate. The field data shows the distribution of the responses of the heads of household selected for the study and indicates that 76% of the respondents were of the opinion that the mining sector does not create equal job opportunities for both the literate and illiterate, with 21% assenting that it does.

Some of those who explained in the affirmative indicated that in some cases illiterates and people with no formal education are employed when mining companies subcontract part of their jobs to other smaller companies and that the few illiterates who are employed are mainly engaged as labourers, those who do the unskilled jobs. On the contrary, however, those who responded in the negative explained that the mining sector, especially the mining companies, employ highly educated and skilled people but not the illiterate and people with very little or no formal education.

Another important area to look at is a group of people whose livelihoods are negatively affected by the mining operations intentionally or unintentionally. As a result, the respondents were asked if they are aware of groups of people who have suffered because of the mining operations in the community. The data indicates that 90 of the respondents out of the 100 responded to this question. The majority of the respondents, constituting 71%, assented to the question while 19% responded in the negative.

When asked to mention some of the suffering, one of those who assented to the question identified that:

> many farmers have lost their livelihoods through the destruction of their farms, those who live very close to the mining sites suffer from frequent 'blasting' and mining waste which pollutes the environment and eventually affects the health of the people.

When the issue of environmental pollution of mining was posed to the Ghana Chamber of Mines in an interview, the official was of the opinion that pollution of the environment was mainly caused by the illegal mining in the country. The official responded that:

> Mining companies also attract illegal mining operations. We need to draw a distinction between 'regulated' and 'non-regulated mining'. It is the unregulated mining that creates most of the environmental challenges.
>
> (Interview with the public relations officer of the Ghana Chamber of Mines, 10 July 2016)

Other respondents said water pollution through the use of chemicals by the mining companies also affects the health of the people. People get dislocated without their due compensation because they live very close to the mining sites.

Further, one other person said 'the physically challenged, the youth, and the illiterate as well as unskilled workers are among the groups of people who have suffered from mining activities'.

Beside this, the respondents were also asked if the mining companies employ natives of the mining communities to its middle to top management positions.

The field data indicates the distribution of their responses and indicates that 89 out of the 100 heads of households responded to this question. The majority of the respondents (64%) assented that natives of the mining companies are employed to the top to middle level management with the 25% responding in the negative.

In their explanations, some of those who responded in the affirmative noted that those who are employed are the highly educated people in the communities and some expatriates but only few natives are employed. For some, even job opportunities for local people are not made public and only those very close to the community leaders get access to such information. On the contrary, some of the people who responded negatively explained that only expatriates occupy the top management and so the people who occupy the middle and top management positions are mainly from outside the mining communities.

Furthermore, the respondents were made to express their opinions about what is to be done to promote the inclusive participation of minority and vulnerable groups in the mining communities. Some of the responses they gave include that there should be a legislation to promote active engagement and inclusive participation of all people in the mining communities.

Again, the mining companies should organise capacity-building programmes to educate and build the technical skills of the people so that they can be made relevant to the mining companies and mining sector for the purposes of job opportunities. Others noted that there should be a legislation to promote transparency and accountability in the mining sector; there should also be adoption of a local content policy to ensure that local community people are employed in the sector. Moreover, others acknowledged that the mining sector should be integrated with other sectors to create jobs, whilst for others people displaced by mining activities should be duly compensated.

4.9 Conclusion

The fieldwork of this book attempts to respond to the objectives of the study, as to how to manage mineral revenues to promote socio-economic development in Ghana. The Western Region of Ghana continues to face challenges in infrastructural development including roads, schools and health facilities despite its mineral wealth. The main occupations of the people in the communities selected for the study are mining and buying and selling or trading. Agriculture, which is the mainstay of the entire Ghanaian economy, occupies a very insignificant part of the communities selected for this study. Consequently, the two sectors, mining and trading, have not created enough jobs for many of the people in such communities, leading to high unemployment rates.

The field data reveals that while education and health continue to receive support from especially mining companies, there are still many challenges in these sectors in the Western Region. Mineral revenues and royalties from central government have not led to significant development in these sectors. The educational system is a caricature of a triangle where the base represents the basic level, which is very broad in access and coverage, but diminishes in numbers and access at the second cycle and tertiary levels. There are very few tertiary institutions in the communities and very high teacher–student ratio, especially at the basic level. The health sector on the other hand also suffers very high doctor–patient ratio with woefully inadequate health facilities, especially in the rural communities of the Western Region.

Based on the field data, community engagement and participation on decisions concerning mining is very minimal and in some cases almost absent, weakening transparency and accountability. In view of this, the mining sector has created unequal job opportunities for especially vulnerable and underprivileged people in the communities.

References

Allen, T., & Thomas, A. (2000). *Poverty and development into the 21st century.* Oxford: Oxford University Press.
Assimeng, M. (1999). *Social structure of Ghana: A study in persistence and change.* Accra: Ghana Publishing Corporation.
Boachie-Danquah, N. (2011). *Reducing corruption at the local government level in Ghana: Decentralization in Ghana.* London: Commonwealth Secretariat.
EITI Report (2016). *Extractive industry transparency initiative annual report.* Accra: Ministry of Finance.

Frank, A.G. (1967). *Capitalism and underdevelopment in Latin America: Historical studies of Chile and Brazil.* New York: Monthly Review Press.

Ghana Statistical Service (2013). *Population census report.* Accra: GSS.

Ghana Statistical Service (2015). *Ghana demographic and health survey.* Accra: GSS.

International Council on Mining and Metals (2015). Report on mining in Ghana: What future can we expect? London: ICMM.

International Monetary Fund (2012). *Ghana poverty reduction strategy paper.* Washington, DC. IMF.

Nukunya, G.K. (2003). *Traditions and change in Ghana: An introduction to sociology,* 2nd edition. Accra: Ghana Universities Press.

Pedro, A.M.A. (2005). *Mainstreaming mineral wealth in growth and poverty reduction strategies: Sustainable development.* Addis Ababa: Economic Commission for Africa.

Pegg, S. (2006). Mining and poverty reduction: Transforming rhetoric into reality. *Journal of Cleaner Production, 14,* 376–387.

Standing, A. (2014). Ghana's extractive industries and commodity benefits sharing: The case for cash transfers. *Resource Policy, 40,* 74–82.

World Bank (2014). *Project performance assessment report.* Washington, DC: World Bank.

UNDP (2011). *Human development report, sustainability and equity: A better future for all.* New York: Palgrave Macmillan.

United Nations (2008). *Principles and recommendations for population and housing census, revision 2.* New York: Department of Economics and Social Affairs, Statistics Division, United Nations.

5 Evaluation of mineral resource governance and human development in Ghana

5.1 Introduction

Creating the right legal regimes for mining can promote economic and human development in Ghana. However, there are currently major challenges facing the mineral governance system in Ghana. The consequences of these challenges have the potential to thwart the development needs of the people. The Western Region of Ghana provides a microcosm of the situation. This chapter presents an in-depth reflection of the findings of the book, substantiated with the development literature. Further, the following subsections summarise the research findings that were investigated in the Western Region of Ghana. The chapter discusses the main issues in the study and how they relate to the overall objectives of the book.

5.2 Quality of living conditions in the Western Region

The Western Region of Ghana is endowed with several mineral resources such as gold, diamond, bauxite and manganese. Although the mining laws indicate that all minerals are for the state, the sector involves foreign mining companies who engage in large-scale mining while the government of Ghana still holds only 10% of identified minerals for commercial exploitation. The small-scale mining industry is, however, reserved for Ghanaians. The small-scale mining industry involves both legal and illegal mining. Despite the mining activities in the Western Region, findings from this study indicate that the majority of the people still live below the international economic poverty line of US$1.9 per day (approximately US$6,935 per annum). This poverty translates into other areas of the households' living conditions. To start with, findings from the communities reveal that majority of the households in the Western Region live in compound houses, which are the most common types of housing in Ghana for low-income earners. Furthermore, 37% of the households in the communities surveyed for the study do not have access to potable water. Out of those who have access to potable water, half of them access water from unimproved sources, making access to potable water one of the major challenges in Ghana.

Furthermore, sanitation poses a challenge to households in Ghana. More than half of the households interviewed do not have their own private decent toilet. This is a common feature of many underprivileged societies in Ghana. Similarly, many households have unhygienic solid waste disposal systems. Less than half of the households adopt hygienic method of waste disposal.

This Mineral Commission of Ghana is the main government agency responsible for the promotion, regulation and management of the utilisation of the mineral resources in the country, as well as the coordination of its policies. In an interview, the Commission was asked to respond to what they perceive to be the development needs of the people. The representative of the Minerals Commission indicated that:

> Their needs are varied. For example, if you go to the Tarkwa, some of the companies annually meet the people in the community and ask them their development needs. They organize durbars. We are a mineral regulation body for government not a development agency. The district assemblies are the development agent in the communities.
>
> (Interview with the manager of sectorial policy and planning, Minerals Commission of Ghana, 4 July, 2016)

Similarly, a representative of WACAM also indicated that:

1. Most of the people in the Western region where the mining is done are farmers. Agricultures should be improved.
2. There should be clear demarcation for areas to be used for mining and areas to be used for agriculture. Most of the areas that are being mined were farmlands, bringing competition between farmlands for agriculture and mining which sometimes results in conflicts in mining areas.
3. People who have been displaced or have their lands taken away from them should be given alternative livelihoods or alternative lands to farm. Some of the development needs of the communities are agriculture, education, health, infrastructural development and supporting people with micro credit.

> (Interview with the public relations officer of
> WACAM, 16 July 2017)

Consequently, it is apparent that majority of the people in the three districts selected for the study live in low-quality conditions. Mining activities have also affected agriculture (which used to be the main occupation of the people) negatively, taking over agricultural lands and rendering many of the people jobless. Moreover, people whose lands have been taken over for mining purposes are not properly compensated, which has discouraged many people from going into agriculture.

Equally important is the seeming disconnection in the working relations between the Minerals Commission of Ghana and the various district assemblies in the mining areas. As a result of this, mining has not been effectively linked with other non-mining sectors to create livelihoods to help improve the standard of living of the people.

5.3 Challenges with human capital formation and skills development

Human capital formation and skills development is crucial in the development of every society. It involves the process of investing in people and increasing the number of people who have the productive qualities and skills, such as the education, skills and health of the labour force. The productive qualities of a people are critical for the socio-economic and political development of a country.

The numbers of educational institutions for training and skills acquisition in Ghana are very small at the tertiary level in relation to the population, but progressively increase in the secondary/high school level and basic level. Vocational and technical institutions, which are supposed to be the training centres for technical capacity-building for the youth, are woefully inadequate. The few available institutions do not equip the students with the requisite skills relevant for mining and other industrial sectors. Further, the current mineral governance arrangement makes it impossible for mining revenues to directly finance education in Ghana. Consequently, funding of education is directly from the Consolidated Fund, which is a pool of funds from the government of Ghana from the different revenue earning sectors of the country's economy. In view of this, funding of education in the Western Region of Ghana is no different from government support to education to other areas where there are no mining activities.

Moreover, the cost of education is high at all levels of the educational ladder. At the basic level, the government has introduced the Free Compulsory Universal Basic Education policy in the public schools, making basic education in the country affordable and accessible. This, however, does not cover the basic private schools making it rather expensive and reserved for mainly middle-income and affluent people. This two-tier education system that prevails in Ghana has ostensibly encouraged social class stratification, where the rich choose one tier and the poor choose another. Basic private schools tend to be effective in terms of teaching, learning and general performance at the Basic Education Certificate Education (BECE) than their counterparts in the public institutions.

At the second cycle level, access is still a challenge; some children who progress from the basic level are unable to progress further to secondary and technical schools. Factors for this include non-qualification as a result of bad grades at the BECE, a woefully inadequate number of secondary schools in relation to the number of students who qualify to be admitted and inability of parents to pay. Although the government of Ghana in 2017 introduced a free senior high school education, some parents still struggle to cater for the living expenses of their children. The second cycle has senior high schools, technical and vocational schools. Out of the three second cycle institutions in Ghana, secondary schools are the most attended by students. This is because the technical and vocational institutions have not received the needed support and attention from government and other stakeholders in the education sector. Many students who graduate from the vocational and technical institutions find it difficult to get tertiary admissions especially into the universities and polytechnics. Quality basic education in the Western Region of Ghana still remains a major challenge with twice as high teacher to student ratio compared with the national average. Besides this, technical and vocational educations have not been properly integrated into the industrial sector, leaving many polytechnic and graduates with technical backgrounds unemployed. On his take on this issue, the mineral resource expert said that 'the few technical institutions in the country have not been well integrated into the industrial sector of the country'.

In the job market, graduates from the polytechnics and people with technical education backgrounds often face huge salary discrimination. University education, on the other hand, remains unaffordable and the privilege of the wealthy few. This is coupled with the fact that there are not many such institutions in the entire country with only one, the University of Mines and Technology, devoted to the study of mining-related issues. This university is situated in the Tarkwa-Nsuaem municipality.

5.4 Challenges with medical care in Ghana

The health of people is an important factor in development. Previous governments of Ghana have implemented several strategies and policies to increase access to quality healthcare at an affordable cost. Despite these efforts, findings from the communities interviewed reveal that Ghana still faces challenges in its health sector. Currently, the country has the National Health Insurance Scheme (NHIS), which replaced the previous 'cash and carry' way of financing healthcare in the country. Nevertheless, the study shows that access to healthcare is still a challenge. The number of health facilities in relation to the population portrays a mismatch as the health facilities are inadequate. The direct consequence of this is the congestion that is often witnessed in the few health facilities (both public and private health institutions). It was revealed from the study that the mining companies do not directly own or run health facilities but do support some of them as part of their corporate social responsibilities. On the issue of affordability of healthcare, the study indicates that many of the people registered under the NHIS are able to afford the cost of healthcare whereas those who are not registered in the NHIS find healthcare very expensive. The study confirmed that most people access healthcare under the government-funded NHIS with only a few who access it under other means such as those under private companies.

Closely associated with access to healthcare is the quality of healthcare. The doctor–patient ratio in Tarkwa Nsuaem is 1:10,053, which is almost the same as the national average of 1:10,170. However, considering the health hazards that mining activities can pose; the doctor to patient ratio is rather on the low side in the mining areas.

5.5 Unemployment in Ghana

Aside revenue generation, employment creation is one of the economic benefits of mining activities. Besides mining, other occupations such as trading and farming are the main occupation of the people in the communities surveyed.

One of the respondents from the communities selected for the study indicated that, 'Mining activities have contributed to the displacement of people from their farmlands and polluted the lands meant for agriculture purposes. Moreover, mining activities have attracted many people, leaving the other sectors of the economy to suffer.' This situation has created a micro-mono-dependent system in the mining areas, a system that has made all the productive activities in the local mining communities evolve around mining. This situation may not, however, apply to the entire country, since Ghana does not depend solely on the extractive sector, but also agriculture and recently crude oil for revenue generation. When asked whether the mining sector has clouded other sectors such as agriculture in the Western Region, an official of the Ghana Chamber of Mines responded:

> Not necessarily. The issue of job sustainability is very critical. The critical question is how we can channel mining resources into other sectors such as such as manufacturing and agriculture to create sustainable jobs. In view of this, every mining company has introduced the 'alternative livelihood programme'. For example, Tarkwa goldfields is into oil palm plantation.
>
> (Interview with the public relations officer of the Ghana Chamber of Mines, 10 July 2016)

On the other hand, trading activities, such as buying and selling are booming in the mining communities, making the sector the second largest employer after the mining sector. Unemployment remains high in Ghana and especially the mining communities and some of the youth adopt every means including illegal means such as unregulated mining just to survive. Findings from the study reveal that mining activities have not created the needed jobs to employ most of the youth in the communities. On his part, a natural resource management expert remarked that:

> Since mining is a capital-intensive sector, not many people can be employed in that sector; therefore, mineral rents should be spent in other sectors that can create jobs. Also it should be spent on the human skills development of the people.
>
> (Interview with a mineral resource expert, University of Ghana, 30 July 2017)

5.6 Transparency and accountability in the mining sector

Transparency and accountability are two very important elements of good governance that promote socio-economic development. These elements cannot exist in isolation but are enforced by institutions and legal frameworks. People in the communities revealed that the mining companies are exploiting them of the resources, leaving them and their communities poor. This perception if not well managed can instigate violence and acrimony between the local people and the mining companies, which are mainly foreign-owned.

Moreover, the respondents revealed that their communities would have been better off without mining. This is simply tied to the structural dependency theory, which explains that the extractions of raw materials by Western countries in their former colonies are detrimental to the development of the local people in these countries (Frank, 1967). Agriculture in particular has suffered due to the destruction of agricultural lands and water bodies by mining activities. The benefits of mining are not clearly evident in the lives of the people in the communities because the revenues are not used in ways that will enhance improvements in the lives of the people. This could be due to the capital-intensive nature of the mining sector, which by nature relies heavily on modern machinery and equipment but less human labour.

One question that begs for answers is how mineral rents can be used to promote socio-economic development. When the official of the Minerals Commission of Ghana was asked on this issue, he responded that;

> We therefore normally tell the local governments that mineral resources are resources that deplete, therefore revenues from it that come to them should be used for sustainable projects such as schools, hospitals and other tangible things so that posterity can appreciate the contribution from mining. So that was a problem we encountered with the District Assemblies, so now the Commission and the Ministry of Finance have given them guidelines for the utilization of mineral revenues since last year 2015. We have also been encouraging the District Assemblies to have a dedicated account for the Mineral revenues that come to them.
> (Interview with the manager of sectorial policy and planning, Minerals Commission of Ghana, 4 July 2016)

The government of Ghana owns, controls and manages the mineral resources on behalf of the people of Ghana. The Minerals and Mining Act of 2006 (Act 703) clearly affirms this. Under the Act, minerals in their natural state, which are in, under or found on Ghana's land, streams, rivers or watercourses are the property of Ghana and are vested in the president of the country in trust for Ghanaians. The president of the Republic of Ghana has the mandate under the Act to compulsorily acquire any land for the utilisation or development of mineral resources. Moreover, the Acts gives power to the minister responsible for that sector the power to act on behalf of the president to 'negotiate, grant, revoke, suspend or renew mineral rights in accordance with the Act' (Act 703, 2006, p. 6).

The community ownership concept of mineral resources, where the local community owns, manages and controls the mineral resources is not likely to work in Ghana. This is because there is a huge mistrust of the local community leaders by the people. The percentage of royalties that goes to the local government and traditional leaders is not spent in a transparent and accountable way. As a result, these local leaders are perceived as corrupt and as liable to misappropriate the funds should the community be given the ownership mandate. Aside this, the local community leaders do not have the competent managerial skills to effectively manage the mining sector. These local leaders include the traditional leaders such as chiefs, queen mothers and other non-traditional leaders including district chief executives, members of Parliament, assembly men and other opinion leaders.

The study revealed that the issue of access to information in the mining sector of Ghana remains a huge challenge. Ghanaians do not have access to information on contractual mining agreements between the government of Ghana and mining companies. On his part, the official of the Minerals Commission responded that:

> People have representatives in Parliament. I'm yet to see a country where the ordinary people are given copies of mining contract agreements. But as a standard practice, when the agreements are made by the attorney general and our legal team, then it goes through Parliament. The people's representative is in Parliament. So, for example, if there is something wrong [it will not benefit the people of Tarkwa] with an agreement between the government of Ghana and AngloGold Ashanti in Tarkwa, the Member of Parliament for Tarkwa is supposed to raise it for it to be addressed in Parliament.
>
> (Interview with the manager of sectorial policy and planning, Minerals Commission of Ghana, 4 July 2016)

Similarly, the study revealed that Ghanaians have no knowledge or information about taxes and royalties paid by mining companies to the government of Ghana and traditional leaders respectively. With specific reference to mining contractual agreements, once Parliament passes the bill, it then becomes a public document and information. Such classified information may be derived from parliamentary Hansards at a fee. Ghana currently does not have a law that gives citizens the right to access classified information from government institutions and organisations. Currently, accessing such classified information from the Parliament of Ghana comes with a fee and not many people are aware of such information and where they can be accessed.

However, when the official of the Ghana Chamber of Mines was asked if they think Ghanaians are aware of how much revenues the mining companies pay to government in the form of corporate tax and as royalties to local traditional leaders, he responded that

Yes, they do. For example, a billboard on the Tetteh Quashie round about that Newmont and Goldfields advertises how much they paid to government in 2015. They publish some in the daily papers. Not all the mining companies do that but Newmont and Goldfields especially do that. The two companies do that in their interest. The Chamber collates data of how much the mining companies paid to government in the form of corporate taxes annually. The data collected aggregates everything, all the taxes together so that for example AngloGold in Obuasi and Tarkwa, people in Obuasi wouldn't know how much exactly was paid in form of taxes.

The EITI is a very good platform for transparency for which the Chamber is a founding member. Here each company reports how much corporate taxes, royalties and property taxes they pay to the government, local assemblies, and regulators. It is published in a report and distributed in the districts. The distribution is done through stakeholder fora where NGOs, civil society organizations are invited.

(Interview with the public relations officer of the
Ghana Chamber of Mines, 10 July 2016)

The Extractive Industry Transparency Initiative (EITI) is sponsored and supported by the UK Department for International Development (DfID). The EITI contains guidelines on how to report mining, oil and gas payments by domestic and international companies to governments. The EITI proposes a data aggregation and analyses methods by an independent third party (Rozner & Gallagher, 2007, p. 34). This means that while the Ghana Chamber of Mines is trying to adopt the EITI, with the aim of promoting transparency and accountability, there still remain challenges about contract agreements. The official of the WACAM responded that:

I agree that the EITI initiative is helping to promote transparency only to some extent. The EITI basically publishes receipts between mining companies and government, but then what about the contract agreements that spell out the amount that these companies are supposed to pay to government? The contract agreements are not made public to the general public, not even the local mining communities.

(Interview with the public relations officer of
WACAM, 16 July 2017)

5.7 Transparency and accountability in the current Minerals and Mining Act 703 (2006)

Transparency and accountability are crucial concepts and initiatives in the mining sector if it is to promote national development. Some of the key stakeholders in the mining sector of Ghana gave their organisations' stance on transparency and accountability.

The following are their responses;

> Transparency we will say is the involvement of all your stakeholders in the involvement of the whole process. It involves inclusiveness, meaning that you are including everybody in the management process as it is prescribed in our laws. And then our subscription to the EITI mining companies should provide information for everybody to see and the reports and publicised for all to see what is coming in and it is used. We subscribe to EITI, and once information is made available it means the first step of accountability has been achieved, because you are providing information about how much revenue comes to government and how it is used. What the EITI aggregator does is that he goes to the mining companies and collects information about how much money, in the form of corporate taxes, royalties and property taxes they pay to government. He then proceeds to the government to get the information about these payments for the purposes of the reconciliation of these payments.
>
> (Interview with the manager of sectorial policy and planning, Minerals Commission of Ghana, 4 July 2016)

> Transparency is showing what you have been able to produce, how much the state is supposed to get out of it based on the agreement we have signed and making sure that everybody knows what went to the actors who are supposed to receive something from the mining process. It starts from contract transparency through the payments to the utilization of revenues. By everybody, I mean Ghanaians. Accountability has to do with what you are supposed to pay, how much you paid and how those proceeds are utilized.
>
> (Interview with the public relations officer of the Ghana Chamber of Mines, 10 July 2016)

> Transparency is about full disclosure of full information with no strings attached. The current Minerals and Mining Act of 2006 (Act 703) restricts the general public from accessing information. People are supposed to pay some money to get information. If you

look at most mining communities where the people are poor, such fees limit their ability to access mining information. Accountability is adopting procedures to give proper information about whatever you are doing and how it affects people.

(Interview with the public relations officer of
WACAM, 16 July 2017)

The above-mentioned conceptions of transparency and accountability underscore the views expressed by Rozner and Gallagher (2007, p. 33) that transparency is 'making information available for the general public'. Accountability in the mining sector means, giving information to the general public about how much taxes and royalties are paid to the government by the mining companies, and reporting on how these proceeds are spent.

The current Minerals and Mining Act of 2006 (Act 703) provides a framework for regulating the mining sector. It clearly indicates how the proceeds from mining should be shared among the various stakeholders. These are central government, local government (district assemblies in mining communities) and local traditional authorities. The breakdown of the proceeds indicated that 80% goes into the Consolidated Fund (a pool of all government funds), 10% goes into another fund (used to support government mineral-related institutions such as the Minerals Commission) and the remaining 10% is shared among the local governments and traditional leaders of mining communities.

However, there is a lacuna in the current Act 703 when it comes to issues of transparency and accountability. The current Minerals Act fails to touch on promoting transparency and accountability and also does not indicate unequivocally how mineral rents should be spent to promote general development. When asked whether there are mechanisms in Act 703 that promote transparency and accountability, the official of WACAM responded:

The Minerals and Mining Act clearly spells out how mineral revenues should be shared; what percentage should go to whom. What is, however, missing from the Act is how those revenues should be used. We don't have a Mineral Revenue Management Act that would regulate the spending of these revenues. This makes proper accountability difficult. If you look at the EITI reports, you will realise that there have been some kinds of reckless spending on the part of government and the local chiefs. Some of the chiefs feel that the monies (royalties) paid to them are for their upkeep.

Furthermore, the EITI also reports that some local governments spend their portion of their royalties on waste management. This makes the calculations difficult. As a result of that the impact of the revenues are not felt by the people.

(Interview with the public relations officer of
WACAM, 16 July 2017)

It is worth noting that in Ghana currently, revenues from minerals are seen and treated as being part of general revenues in the Consolidated Fund. Money from the Consolidated Fund is used by government to run its day-to-day business as well as being invested in other sectors of the county's economy. This practice dilutes the important contribution of mining in the eyes of the general public and also does not convert revenues from minerals into sustainable human development interventions. In the utilisation of the fund, no regional considerations or community considerations are given; as such, people from mining communities are not given preferential treatment.

One other important area to focus attention on is the management of these resources and how they are used, especially the percentage that goes to the communities. Findings from the communities selected for this study revealed that most Ghanaians, especially those in mining communities, do not feel that they benefit from the proceeds of mining or that proceeds from the mining are invested judiciously in interventions that directly or indirectly benefit them. On his part, the official of the Minerals Commission of Ghana was asked if he agrees to the assertion held by the people that mineral rents are not utilised responsibly. He responded that:

Yes, I do. They normally refer to it at recurrent expenditure, and sometimes they use part of the money to collect waste. We therefore normally tell them that mineral resources deplete, therefore revenues from it that come to them should be used for sustainable projects such as schools, hospitals and other tangible things so that posterity can appreciate the contribution from mining. So that was a problem we encountered with the District Assemblies, so now the Commission and the Ministry of Finance have given them guidelines for the utilization of mineral revenues since last year 2015. We have also been encouraging the District Assemblies to have a dedicated account for the Mineral revenues that come to them.

(Interview with the manager for sectorial policy and
planning, Minerals Commission of Ghana, 4 July 2016)

The guidelines for the utilisation of the mineral revenues are not backed by law and therefore do not compel the leaders who manage these resources on how the rents should be used.

Equally important to the study is the issue of equitable participation by various members of Ghanaian society. Equitable participation has become one of the definitions of the concept of development. This is even more so since almost all known societies are made up of heterogeneous compositions in the form of social differences and social stratification in terms of gender, age, level of education, wealth, power, prestige and privilege, among others (Nukunya, 2003). These social differences have led to unequal access to the various social goods and services in society. On the issue of gender, the study revealed that while the mining sector employs both men and women, the sector is male-dominated in terms of employment.

Similarly, vulnerable people such as physically challenged people are denied opportunities to work in the mining sector. Whereas the Ghana Chamber of Mines indicates that the mining sector of Ghana is an equal opportunity sector, the findings from the study revealed that the sector is biased towards able-bodied people.

Employment opportunities in the mining sector favour very educated people whose qualifications are related to the work demands in the mining sector. Rarely do uneducated people get the opportunity to work in the sector. Most of the time when they do, it is normally in the small mining companies (with most of them operating illegally). There is little or no training for unskilled people who want to work in the sector, especially in the large-scale mining companies. Employment is sometimes not based on merit. Most of the time, even among highly educated and qualified people, there is the need to 'connect' to someone in a top management position, either politically, in local traditional leadership or at the top level management of the mining companies, in order to get employment in the sector.

On the issue of mining and pollution, one of the respondents said that;

> We can't go into farming in this area because the chemicals used for the mining activities have led to the pollution of the land and water bodies. The few who dared to venture into it have had problems with low yields and some also have their farmlands taken over by both legal and illegal miners.

Mining activities have contributed to the environmental pollution of the mining communities. Chemicals that are used can be hazardous to people's health and also lead to the pollution of farmlands. This has contributed to the displacement of farmers and homeowners, especially in areas with mineral deposits. Many such people have complained of lack of accountability on the part of mining companies in paying compensation to them.

5.8 Conclusion

This chapter presents an in-depth reflection of the findings of the study. The quality of living conditions in the Western Region of Ghana is poor. Furthermore, both education and healthcare continue to face serious challenges in areas of quality, access and affordability. Unemployment continues to pose a major challenge, with some youth in the Western Region resorting to illegal mining, which ends up destroying the environment. Ghana's mining sector continues to suffer from lack of transparency and accountability since the country's Minerals and Mining Act 703 of 2006 does not address these issues. As a result, this does not ensure the judicious use of mineral revenues for human development.

References

Frank, A.G. (1967). *Capitalism and underdevelopment in Latin America: Historical studies of Chile and Brazil.* New York: Monthly Review Press.
Minerals and Mining Act 703 (2006). Accra: Minerals Commission of Ghana.
Nukunya, G.K. (2003). *Traditions and change in Ghana: An introduction to sociology*, 2nd edition. Accra: Ghana Universities Press.
Rozner, S., & Gallagher, M. (2007). Tools for treating the resource curse. *Developing Alternatives*, 11(1), 28–34.

6 Human-centred mineral resource governance approach

6.1 Introduction

This chapter engages the human-centred mineral resource governance approach and discussed how it can apply to Ghana and other mineral wealth sub-Saharan countries. Despite its mineral wealth, Ghana and many other mineral wealth sub-Saharan African countries still face development challenges. Although the rent-seeking government theory and the revisionist theory of natural resources attempt to explain the relationship between mineral resources and development, they do not explain Ghana's situation. As a result, the human-centred mineral resource governance approach attempts to respond to the following research questions:

1. How can Ghana and other mineral wealth sub-Saharan African countries govern their mineral resource sector to promote transparency and accountability?
2. How judiciously can mineral rents be utilised to promote human development in Ghana?
3. In what ways can the mineral sector in Ghana be structured to promote equitable participation by citizens of mineral rich countries?

Unlike the rent-seeking government theory, findings from this study confirm that effective governance of mineral resources can promote socio-economic development in Ghana. In order to achieve this and respond to the above questions, the human-centred mineral resource governance approach puts forward the following.

6.2 Legalising policies to promote transparency and accountability

Mineral resources and resource revenues can be effectively managed when the government of Ghana takes well-advised decisions. Such

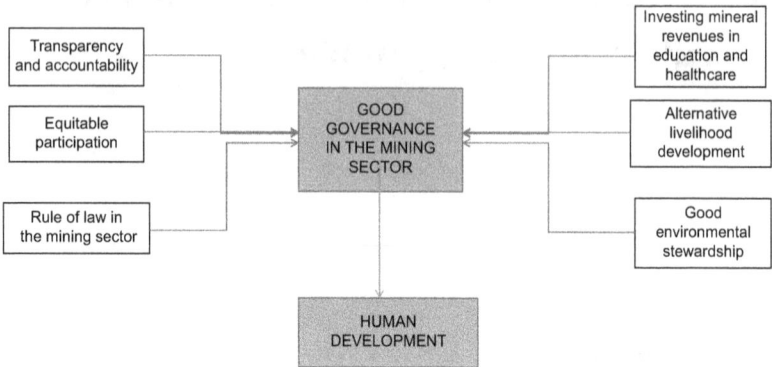

Figure 6.1 Human-centred mineral resource governance approach.

good decisions emerge and are sustained in an atmosphere of scrutiny and accountability, reinforced by transparency and the availability of relevant information in the mining sector. Accordingly, the government of Ghana should legalise regulations that will promote transparency and accountability. If transparency mechanisms are introduced in the decision-making chain throughout the mining cycle, it can promote government accountability to the various stakeholders in the Ghanaian mining industry. Effective accountability can be achieved through transparency if the citizens, who are the owners of the mineral resources, are able to use the existing information to monitor to the actions of their government. The government of Ghana should therefore establish mechanisms that will promote meaningful stakeholder engagement, systems that can monitor the use of mineral resources and a platform where claims of negative large mining effects on the people and communities where they operate can be assessed.

Besides, making information (such as revenue data, tax rates, volumes of production and taxable income) accessible to the citizens throughout the mining cycle will ensure that the government of Ghana remains accountable to its citizens as well as all the other stakeholders in the mining industry and will help to promote the efficient use of mineral rents and reduce corruption. The lack of transparency and accountability in Ghana's mining sector has contributed greatly to the upsurge of illegal mining activities. A recent secret investigation by the Bureau of National Investigations of Ghana revealed that prominent actors in the country's development, including members of Parliament, top politicians (from the two main political parties), top security officials, local chiefs (especially in mining areas) and opinion leaders were all mentioned as actively engaging in illegal and unregulated mining.

Currently, Ghana's Parliament is considering the passage of the Right to Information Bill, which, when passed, will contribute enormously to the enhancement of transparency across all sectors. While the bill is waiting to be passed, government can enhance transparency by disclosing mining contracts to the general public. Keeping it confidential can generate mistrust, promote conflicts and raise the expectation of the general public, especially the local mining communities.

6.3 Introducing laws and policies on the utilisation of mineral revenues

The current structure in Ghana where mineral revenues are treated as part of general revenues that go into the Consolidated Fund and are spent indiscriminately by the government dilutes the contribution of the mining sector in the eyes of the general public and does not ensure that mineral revenues are spent on sustainable human-centred interventions for Ghana's development. As a result, the government of Ghana should introduce a Mineral Revenue Management Act, to serve as a legal framework that will determine how mineral revenues should be spent.

Moreover, since mineral resources deplete, it is prudent to invest in people-centred interventions such as education, health and job creation to create sustainable returns. Consequently, for mineral resources to promote the sustainable quality of life and well-being of Ghanaians, it must be human-centred. Critical human-centred development areas that the government of Ghana should invest mineral revenues in are education, health and job creation.

In the area of education, the government of Ghana should invest mineral revenues in the construction of educational institutions. In particular, at the tertiary level, investments in the construction of at least two universities in each region of the country will contribute enormously towards the training of professionals for the country. Technical and vocational institutions already existing in Ghana must be given face-lifts and linked with the industrial sector of the country's economy. There should be training of more teachers across the various levels of the educational ladder and the provision of incentives for teachers who accept postings to deprived communities of the country. In order that the coverage of education in Ghana can be universal, the Ghanaian government should channel resources in the provision of scholarships for needy students at all levels.

Besides this, the government of Ghana must invest mineral revenues in the construction of more health facilities and train more health personnel to cater for the current deficit in the health sector. This will help to improve access and quality healthcare in Ghana. The National Health Insurance Scheme, which is currently facing financial challenges, can be supported with mineral revenues so as to tackle the current challenge of access and affordability in the health sector of Ghana.

If mineral revenues are invested in these areas, it will help to solve the numerous challenges in the education and health sectors while contributing to the creation of jobs to address the current unemployment situation in Ghana.

6.4 Encouraging active participation of stakeholders throughout the mine life cycle

Participatory development ensures that stakeholders are able to influence development initiatives and make contributions to decisions and resources that affect them.

Ghana has vibrant civil society organisations (CSOs) that represents the general public. The contribution of these CSOs in consolidating political development in the country has been enormous. Since 1992, Ghana has held six different highly contested successful political elections every four years, with power swinging three times between the two main political parties (New Patriotic Party and National Democratic Congress). There are both national and international CSOs in the mining sector, operating at both local and national levels. Currently, the system does not give the CSOs a more active and formal voice in the mining sector as it does in the political sector. The government of Ghana as a lead stakeholder should encourage the active inclusive involvement of the general public through their representatives at the various levels of the mining cycle, starting from contract negotiations to how mineral revenues are spent. This will help to promote transparency and accountability. The general public will be in a better position to understand and contribute to the mining industry; such as the mining life cycle, the community legal rights in the mining sector and how the Ghanaian government (both central and local) as well as local traditional leaders entrusted with mineral revenues can judiciously utilise the revenues to promote the socio-economic development of the country. This will also contribute greatly to managing the expectations of the general public, especially at the local level where mining activities are done.

Furthermore, effective stakeholder engagement in the mining sector of Ghana can ensure that mining companies go beyond minimum legal requirements in the execution of their operations and ensure their diligence, so that they can identify, avert and mitigate against possible human rights infringements.

6.5 Developing a comprehensive local content policy

The government of Ghana should link the mining sector to the broader industrial sector by increasing local procurement. This will not only help in deepening the linkages of the mining sector with other non-mining sectors but also contribute to the creation of jobs and the general expansion of the country's economy.

Non- mining sectors such as banking and insurance sector, metal works services, pumps and spares, chemicals used for mining, light manufacturing in cyanide, catering services among others can all be strategically linked to the mining sector. Investors are considerably more attracted to a very strong local industry with employees who have the requisite technical and vocational skills.

Furthermore, such proposed policy should also address employment for Ghanaian local people. Most of the youth especially in the local mining communities are unskilled with low formal education making their employment difficult. Such local content policy must be inclusively participatory by particularly identifying and empowering socially marginalised members of the Ghanaian society such as women, the physically challenged as well as unskilled people who are normally either entirely socially marginalised or subordinately included in the development process. The government of Ghana as a leading stakeholder in the mining industry, the Ghana Chamber of Mines and other stakeholders should collaborate in training and building the capacities of such people so that they can take advantage of available opportunities in the mining sector.

6.6 Developing alternative livelihood strategies

The study revealed that mining activities have taken over farmlands and other agricultural activities leading to an almost collapse of the agricultural sector in the mining communities, which previously was the mainstay of the Ghanaian economy. Consequently, the government of Ghana should consider collaborating with other stakeholders to develop alternative livelihood strategies especially in mining communities, particularly in areas of agriculture, manufacturing and other small and medium-sized enterprises.

In addition, many local communities where mining is done in Ghana are heavily dependent on the mining sector for jobs and other opportunities, creating mono-economies in many of these communities. In order to avert this problem, the government of Ghana should introduce a comprehensive development programme linked with the alternative livelihood strategies to diversify the economies of local mining communities so as to create sustainable jobs and human development.

In some cases, farming lands are taken over for mining activities by mining companies in Ghana. Although some of the affected farmers get compensated, there are often complaints of discontentment by these farmers. Some get discouraged from investing back into agriculture. To address this problem, the government of Ghana, using geological information, should clearly demarcate mining areas from non-mining areas and ensure strict compliance to laws regulating such demarcations.

The government of Ghana and other stakeholders must take a keen interest in training more teachers and health personnel especially in mining communities since these professions are in high demand in the country. Similarly, there should be active engagement and training of the women and the youth, especially those denied a formal education to develop their capacities and equip them with income generation skills such as to be artisans and own their businesses.

6.7 Promoting better environmental stewardship

Mining activities in Ghana are having devastating environmental consequences in the local mining communities, such as pollution of water bodies, pollution of air, noise pollution and the destruction of farmlands. The Ghanaian government, mining companies and civil society organisations (CSOs) have critical roles to play in preventing, mitigating and offsetting the negative impacts of mining and improve opportunities for development.

The study discovered that Ghana has comprehensive environmental laws contained in the Environment Protection Agency's bylaws, such as regulations on who can mine, where mining should be done, and regulations on environmentally sustainable mining processes to safeguard the environment; however, environmental pollution in many mining communities is still rampant. In order to avert this problem of mining, the government should strictly enforce these environment bylaws to enhance environmental stewardship.

One way the government of Ghana can ameliorate this challenge is to introduce environmental bonds. Environmental bonds, which are financial arrangements between a regulator (in this case, the Environmental Protection Agency of Ghana) and the resource developers (mining companies), provide financial surety against the possible negative environmental effects of mining activities on local communities. This will help the government and the mining communities to reduce the risks, should the mining companies fail to comply with the legal environmental bylaws.

Perhaps one of the biggest causes of environmental pollution in the mining sector is the management of liquid and solid wastes. The ineffective management of mineral wastes can create a perpetual source of pollution. The government of Ghana should encourage mining companies and their associated bodies (in particular, the Ghana Chamber of Mines) to conduct research into new technologies and strategies for improved management of mineral wastes.

In summary, the current Minerals and Mining Act (703) of 2006 is the main framework that regulates the mining sector of Ghana and clearly indicates how the mineral revenues should be shared. Conspicuously missing from the Act are good governance issues; however, introducing sound governance policies in the mining sector is one of the surest ways to promote human development. This is because good governance is likely to enhance effective and efficient use of mineral revenues and is more likely to ensure that Ghanaians benefit from the mineral resources.

Pertinent issues of transparency, accountability, inclusive participation and sustainable development are needed if the mining sector can respond to the current human development challenges Ghana faces.

Legalising policies to promote transparency, integrating mining into national development and poverty reduction strategies while prioritising issues of education, health and job creation are particularly important steps to ensure that Ghana beats the resource curse. This is the surest way mineral resources can promote people-centred development in Ghana.

Reference

Minerals and Mining Act 703 (2006). Accra: Minerals Commission of Ghana.

Index

Note: Page numbers in *italics* indicate figures and tables.

access: to education 67–70, 99–100;
to healthcare 74–7, 101, 114; to
information on mining sector 8,
88–90, 104–5, 106–7, 112, 113; to
job opportunities via community
leaders 94, 109; to safe drinking
water 65, 98; unequal access to
goods/services in society 92, 109
accountability: overview/definitions
of 17–18, 107; in 2006 Minerals
and Mining Act 106–7; in budget
formulation/implementation
37; calls for promotion of via
legislation 91, 94; Chamber of
Mines official's views on 106;
criticism of state's weak political
accountability 14; and importance
of high literacy rates 59; lacking in
chiefs' utilisation of revenues 12,
85, 88, 104; lacking in payment of
compensation for pollution 110;
lacking in policy on MDF 11;
linked to benefits from resource
wealth 33; Minerals Commission
official's views on 106; needs
reinforcing in mining sector 8, 105,
112, 117; as part of human-centred
resource governance approach 112,
112; pivotal to good governance
30, 83, 102; promoted via EITI
105; promoted via stakeholder
engagement in mining sector 114;
Revenue Watch Institute, work of

39; WACAM official's views on
107; *see also* transparency
Acosta, M.A. 17, 18, 19
Adimazoya, T.N. 8
Administration of Lands Act
(1962) 6
affordability: of education 70–2,
99–100, *100*; of healthcare 77, 101,
114; *see also* cost of living
Africa: crucial role of family in 54–5;
elites benefitting from mineral
resources 4; huge natural resource
base in 26–7; paradox of the
'resource curse' in 1; patriarchal
view of male dominance over
women 55–6
African Development Bank *13*, 26–7
age: of household heads 56; of
school-going children 71, *72*
agricultural sector: and employment,
as source of 2, 27, 61, 82, 101;
farming as main occupation
of respondents 79, 101; and
income, as source of 61; mining
sector's impact on 79–80, 82, 93,
99, 101–2, 103, 109–10, 115–16,
116; as percentage of occupation
of household heads 60; and
reasons for non-transformative
development of Ghana 25;
rents from peasant farming 21;
WACAM official's views on 98
artisan mining 5, 27

Aryee, B.N.A 2
audits 12, 86
Australia 9, 26, 27
authoritarianism 23
autocracies 31–2
Auty, R.M. 1, 20, 21
Azerbaijan 37

Bank of Ghana 3, *13*
Barnett, S. 40
Basic Education Certificate
    Examination 73, 100
basic (primary) education 59, 68, 69,
    70, 99, 100
bauxite 2, 5, 7, 9, 28, *48*, 84
Blair, Tony 38
Boachie-Danquah, N. 88
Botswana 25, 26, 33, 35
bribes 81
Britain *see* United Kingdom
budgets: civil society initiatives 36,
    37–8; and Fiscal Transparency
    Code of Good Practices 38
Bureau of National Investigations of
    Ghana 112–13
Buur, L. 26

Canada 9, 26, 27
capacity-building 11, 20, 34, 37, 38,
    94, 115
Capital Development Fund 40
Carmody, P. 4
case study methodology 46–52;
    see also heads of households;
    households; Western Region
    of Ghana
cash transfers 33–4, 34–5
Centre on Budget and Policy
    Priorities 38
Chad 36, 39
Chamber of Mines *see* Ghana
    Chamber of Mines
chemicals, use of 94, 109–10, 115;
    see also environment: negative
    impact of mining on
chiefs *see* traditional authorities
children: and composition of case
    study households 60; mortality
    rates of 32, 74, 77–8; and school
    attendance 71, 72

Christian religion 58
Citizen's Guide (Schultz) 38–9
civil marriages 58
civil society organisations:
    budget initiatives 36, 37–8;
    involvement in governance
    29, 30, 31; participation in
    poverty reduction strategies
    36, 37; role in consolidating
    political development 114; role
    in militating against effects
    of resource curse 33; role in
    prevention of mining pollution
    116; *see also* non-governmental
    organisations (NGOs)
civil wars 23
clinics 75, *75*
cocoa exports 3
Collier, P. 24, 33
colonial mining policy 5
Commission of Enquiry into
    Concessions 5–6
communities: and access to
    information on mineral revenues
    8, 89–90, 104, 105, 112, 113; and
    aims of colonial mining policy
    5; and citizens' perceptions of
    exploitation by mining companies
    102; development of via MDF
    2, 7, 10, *10*, 11; development
    of via mineral revenues 1, 12,
    27, 40, 67, 83, 84–6, 87–8, 91,
    103, 108, 117; and distribution
    of natural resources rents 34;
    and dominance of men over
    women in households 55–6; and
    environmental impact of mining
    on development of 82; lack of
    state's engagement with 14; and
    mining companies' profit-making
    vs community development
    81–2, 82–3; need for capacity-
    building of 20; need to participate
    in mining sector 88, 91, 94,
    114–15, 117; and ownership/
    control of mineral resources
    86, 87–8, 103–4, 112; as player
    in mining sector *13*; as primary
    and legitimate stakeholder
    14; and recommendations of

Commission of Enquiry 6; role as 'watchdogs' 37; and utilisation of Consolidated Fund 108; *see also* heads of households
community-based health planning services (CHPS) 75, *75*
compensation payments 99, 110, 116
compliance 18, 116
composition of households 60
compound houses 62, 63, 97–8
concessions 5–6
conflicts 23–4, 31
Consolidated Fund 10, *10*, 11, 99, 107, 108, 113
constitution of Ghana 8, 58
contracts *see* mining contracts
control of mineral resources 86–7, 87–8, 103–4
corruption 23, 32, 84, 88, 91, 104, 112
cost of living: linked to household size 60; and need to find work 61; and unaffordability of basic needs 62; and utilisation of mineral resources 84, 85; *see also* affordability
customary marriages 58

Daniel, J. 40
data: centralised nature of 47; primary and secondary data sources 50–1
data collection: methodology used in case study 46, 49–51; state of Ghana as unit of 51
Davis, G. 25, 27
Davis, J. 40
democracy: connection to economic and social development 28; and correlation between authoritarianism and natural resources 23; and correlation with resource curse 33, 35; lacking in autocracies 32; natural resource wealth as obstacle to 22; and 'repression effect' of rents 22–3; situation in Ghana 25; *see also* entries under governance
demographic information on households 54–62; *see also* heads of households

Department for International Development (UK) *13*, 35, 38
developing countries: connection between politics and economy 20; public health as neglected aspect of development 66; use of natural resources for development 26
development: and citizens' knowledge/awareness of NGOs 90–1; concept of equitable participation important in 92, 109; enhanced by human-centred approach 113; and issues around governance 30–1, 33; Minerals Commission official's views on 98; Minerals Development Fund 2, 7, 10, *10*, 11; and mining companies' profit-making 81–2, 82–3; and mining sector's contributions to 1, 12, 27, 40, 67, 83, 84–6, 87–8, 91, 103, 108, 117; and negative environmental impact of mining on 82; and NGOs' critiques of government policies 14; non-transformative development of Ghana 25; rent-seeking/revisionist theories' explanations of 111; skewed patterns in mineral wealth countries 32–3; skills development 67, 94, 99, 102; social development 1, 27, 28, 32, 40, 83; structural dependency theory views on 81–2, 102–3; sustainable development 27, 31, 67, 87–8, 117; use of mineral rents in development interventions 21; WACAM official's views on 98; World Bank report on Ghanaian government's efforts 11, 82; *see also* economic development; human development; Minerals Development Fund (MDF); socio-economic development
diamonds 2, 5, 7, 28, *48*, 84
disabled persons 92, 94, 109, 115
diseases 65
district assemblies: critical role in governance of mining sector 12; as development agent in communities 98; disbursements of revenues to *10*, 11, 12, 85–6, 103, 107, 108; and

disconnection in relations with Minerals Commission 99; mandate of 8; misappropriation of revenues 86, 104; as player in mining sector 13, *13*
dividends 2
divorce 57
doctors 78, 101
document reviews, as data collection instrument 49, 51
donors 30–1
Dutch disease 24

Eastern religions 58
economic development: and correlation between industrialisation and natural resources 26; correlation with education 67; correlation with natural resources 20, 24, 24–5, 27; impact of transfer through pricing strategy on 34; and lower growth theory 25, 26; mining sector's contribution to 1; *see also* development; resource curse
Economic Recovery Programme 6–7, *7*
economic rents 20, 21
education: access to 67–70, 99–100; affordability of 70–2, 99–100, *100*; and employment opportunities in mining sector 59, 93, 94, 109, 115; level of education of household heads 59; as measure of human development 66–7; need for human-centred mineral governance approach to *112*, 113; quality of 72–4, 100
elections in Ghana 114
electricity connection 63–5, 65, 88
elites: and appropriation of natural resource wealth 4, 20–1, 35–6; and political situation in Ghana 25
employment: agricultural sector as source of 2, 27, 61, 82, 101; enabled via connections to community leaders 94, 109; and equitable participation in mining sector 92–3, 94, 109, *112*; and importance of local content

policy 115; job creation via rent distribution 34; mining sector as source of 2–3, 4, 20, 27, 61, 79–81, 83, 84, 101, 102; need for alternative livelihood strategies 115–16; need for human-centred mineral governance approach to *112*, 113; opportunities increased via education 59, 93, 94, 109, 115; and salary discrimination 100; *see also* job creation; unemployment
energy sources 65
enrolment in schools 69–70
environment: need for human-centred mineral governance approach to *112*; negative impact of mining on 80, 82, 84, 93, 94, 101, 103, 109–10, 116–17; value of environmental bonds 116–17
Environmental Protection Agency 11, 116
equity: equitable participation in mining employment 92–3, 94, 109, *112*; as indicator for good governance 30; in mineral governance 18–19
European Commission 29, 30
examinations 73, 100
exports: of cocoa/oil 3; contribution of natural resources to 27; correlation with potential for conflicts 24; gold as primary export 2, 3; impact of dependence on export of primary products 21; recommendations of Commission of Enquiry 6
extended family system 54, 54–5, 60
Extractive Industries Transparency Initiative (EITI) *13*, 38, 90, 105, 106, 107–8
extractive sector 4, 20, 101; *see also* mining sector

fairness in mineral resource use 19
family, role of 54–5
farming *see* agricultural sector
fees: for accessing mining information 104, 106–7; for schooling 71–2, 99–100
financial audits 12, 86

fiscal pacts 36
Fiscal Transparency Code of Good
    Practices 38
fishing sector 79
foreign aid rents 20
foreign direct investment 27
foreign exchange resources 3
foreign mining companies 97, 102
'formation effect' of rents 22
Free Compulsory Universal Basic
    Education policy 67, 71, 99–100
Friedman, Thomas 32
funding: of education 69, 99; of
    Minerals Commission 107;
    proposal for Capital Development
    Fund 40; proposal for mining
    community development fund 83

Gallagher, M. 35–6, 36, 37, 38, 39,
    40, 41, 107
gender: distribution of case study
    respondents 55; and dominance
    of men over women 55–6; and
    equitable participation in mining
    sector employment 92, 109
Geological Surveys Department 13
Ghana: abundance of mineral
    deposits in 2; Bureau of National
    Investigations 112–13; classified
    by IMF as mineral wealth country
    2; elections in 114; historical
    overview of mineral policies 5–7;
    place in Transparency Index 8;
    political situation in 25; poverty in
    4, 97–8; as unit of data collection/
    analysis in case study 51; *see also*
    government of Ghana; Western
    Region of Ghana
Ghana Chamber of Mines: adoption
    of EITI 105; claim that mining
    sector is equal opportunity sector
    109; interviews with officials from
    50, 80, 89–90, 93, 102, 104–5, 106;
    need for local content policy 115;
    as player in mining sector *13*
Ghana Revenue Authority 3
gold mining: 40% of reserves found
    in Africa 1; contributes more than
    90% of minerals 7–8; household
    heads' knowledge about 84; major

companies in Ghana *9*; one of
    Ghana's primary exports 2, 3
governance: overview of concept/
    definitions of 28–30; and access
    to job opportunities 92; as factor
    in development debates 30–1;
    impact of mineral wealth on good
    governance 23; and revisionist
    theory of natural resource
    development 31–41; transparency/
    accountability pivotal to 30, 31, 83,
    102; *see also* democracy
governance of mineral resources:
    definitions and conceptualisation
    of 5, 17–20; and citizens' access to
    information on mining contracts
    8, 88–9; and contributions of
    revenues to education 99; human-
    centred approach to 111, *112*,
    113, 117; institutional and legal
    framework 7–12; linked to human
    development 46, 54, 117; occurs
    in a set of policy and regulatory
    structures 51; and ownership/
    control of mineral resources 86–7;
    and promotion of socio-economic
    development 111, 114
government of Ghana: actions to
    attract investment in mining sector
    7; appointment of Commission of
    Enquiry 5–6; and citizens' access
    to information on mining sector
    8, 88–90, 104–5, 106–7, 112, 113;
    holds only 10% of minerals for
    commercial exploitation 97; need
    for local content policy 115; need
    for Mineral Revenue Management
    Act 85, 107, 113; needs to
    encourage stakeholder engagement
    in mining sector 114; and
    ownership/control/management
    of mineral resources 6, 86, 87,
    103, 111–12; payment of mining
    revenues to 10; role in prevention
    of mining pollution 116–17; role in
    regulation of mining sector 12–13,
    98; as source of education funding
    69; and use of Consolidated Fund
    10, *10*, 11, 99, 107, 108, 113; World
    Bank report on efforts to utilise

mineral revenues 11, 82; *see also*
Ghana; Minerals Commission of
Ghana; Parliament
gross domestic product (GDP) 1, 2,
20, 21, 24
Guatemala 36
Gylfason, T. 23, 24

Hartwick's rule 39, 40
heads of households: and case study,
data collection methods used in
46, 49, 50, 51; and case study,
rationale for inclusion in 47, 49;
demographic information on
54–62; educational issues, views
on 67–74; equitable participation
in mining sector employment,
views on 92–3, 94; healthcare
issues, views on 75–9; housing
conditions and well-being of
62–6; job opportunities in mining
sector, views on 79–83; knowledge
of mineral resources 83–91; main
occupations of 79, 101; *see also*
households
healthcare: in Ghana's Western
Region 74–9, 100–1; need for
human-centred mineral governance
approach to *112*, 113; need for
training of personnel 114, 116;
public health as measure of socio-
economic status 66
Hoeffler, A. 24, 33
hospitals 75, *75*, 79
households: definition of 47;
geographical distribution of case
study 47, *48*, 49; *see also* heads of
households
housing conditions 62–3, 97–8
human-centred mineral resource
governance 111, *112*, 113, 117
human development: development
of human capital 25, 40, 66,
99–100; education as vital tool
for 59, 66–7, 70; electricity supply
essential for 64; energy sources
as indicator of 65; healthcare as
crucial determinant of 74; linked
to mineral governance 46, 54,
117; measures of 4; vs mineral

resource management 4; and need
for alternative livelihood strategies
115–16; need for human-centred
resource governance approach
to *112*; occurs within policy and
regulatory structures 51; sanitation
as neglected aspect of 66; and
utilisation of Consolidated Fund
108; *see also* development
hydrocarbon-rich countries 31–2, 32

illegal mining 74, 80, 81, 93, 97, 102,
109, 112–13
illiteracy 93, 94
inclusivity: as indicator for good
governance 31; in mineral
governance 18; need for inclusive
participation in mining sector 94,
117; *see also* participation
income, sources of 61–2
income taxes 2, 5, 7; *see also* taxation
independent media 33
Indonesia 34
industrial minerals 7
industrial sector 21, 26, 100, 113, 115
infant mortality rates 32, 74, 77–8
information, access to 8, 88–90,
104–5, 106–7, 112, 113
institutional framework of mining
sector 7–12
insurance health schemes 74, 76, 76–
7, 77, 101, 114
International Budget Project 38
International Council on Mining and
Metals 11, 79, 82
International Monetary Fund (IMF):
adoption of Fiscal Transparency
Code of Good Practices 38;
classification of mineral wealth
countries 2; launch of ERP 7;
poverty reduction strategy 12, 36, 86
interviews: as data collection
instrument 46, 51; with Ghana
Chamber of Mines officials 50, 80,
89–90, 93, 102, 104–5, 106; with
Minerals Commission of Ghana
officials 50, 85–6, 89, 98, 103, 104,
106, 108; with University of Ghana
experts 67, 102; with WACAM
officials 50, 90, 98, 105, 106–7, 107–8

job creation: necessity to spend mineral rents on 67, 102; need for alternative livelihood strategies 115–16; and need for integration of economic sectors 94; of non-market support jobs 21; in sectors other than mining 80, 83, 84; strategies in Indonesia 34; via development of local content policy 115; via investment in health facilities 114; *see also* employment

Kaplan, D. 26
Kaplinsky, R. 26
Kauzya, J.M. 30, 31
kindergartens 68, 69

labour: skilled labour 25, 80–1, 93, 109; unskilled/manual labour 60, 81, 93, 94, 109, 115
law *see* legislation on mining
leadership 31, 84, 88, 91, 109
leases, award of 8
legal framework of mining sector 7–12
legislation on mining: Administration of Lands Act 6; and calls for inclusive participation of mining communities 94, 117; calls for Mineral Revenue Management Act 85, 107, 113; and calls for transparency/accountability in mining sector 91, 94; indication that all minerals are for the state 97; Minerals Act 6, 6–7; Minerals and Mining Act 7, 8, 10, 10–11, 12, 14, 103, 106–7, 117; Minerals and Mining Amendment Act 10; Minerals and Mining Law 7; as part of human-centred mineral resource governance *112*
licences, award of 8
lighting, sources of 64, 64–5
literacy 59, 73–4, 93
living conditions in Western Region 97–9; *see also* cost of living; standard of living
Lledo, V. 36
local content policy 81, 94, 115

local government 13, 30, 31, 89, 90, 103, 104, 107, 108; *see also* district assemblies; government of Ghana
lower growth theory 25, 26

management of mineral resources: communities' potential role in 87–8, 103–4; Ghanaian government's role in 6, 87, 111–12; vs human development 4; provisions of Minerals Act 6; *see also* mineral resources
management of natural resources, revisionist theory of 25–41, 111
managerial sector 60, 61, 94, 109
manganese 2, 5, 7, *9*, 28, 84
manual/unskilled labour 60, 81, 93, 94, 109, 115
marriage: marital status of household heads 56–7; types of 57–8
matrilineal families 54
media, independent 33
medical care *see* healthcare
Meissner, H. 22
men: and composition of case study households 60; and equal opportunities in mining employment 92, 109; as heads of households 55, 56
methodology of case study research 46–52
Millennium Development Goals 67
mineral policies 5–7, 51
mineral rents/revenues: allocated to district assemblies *10*, 11, 12, 85–6, 103, 107, 108; allocated to traditional authorities *10*, 11, 12, 104, 105, 107, 107–8; allocation to MDF 11; in autocracies 32; citizens' access to information on 104–5, 112; contributions to education 67–8, 68, 69, 73–4, 82, 99, 113, 114; contributions to healthcare 78–9, 101, 113, 114; form part of general revenues in Consolidated Fund 108, 113; importance of spending on human skills development 67, 102; invested in various parts of Ghanaian economy 2; and

legislative regulation of 107, 117; management of as tool to tackle resource curse 35; Minerals Commission official's views on benefits of 85–6, 103; need for human-centred governance approach to 111–12; need for Mineral Revenue Management Act 85, 107, 113; and need for stakeholder engagement in mining sector 114; participation as tool in prevention of misuse of 35–6; in promotion of community development 1, 12, 27, 40, 67, 83, 84–6, 87–8, 91, 103, 108, 117; proposal for Capital Development Funds 40; and Publish What You Pay initiative 39; quarterly payments to Ghanaian government 10; as significant source of Ghana's foreign exchange resources 3; and skewed development patterns 32–3; strategies for spending 33–4; three main types of 20–1; tools for monitoring of 38–9; tools of macro fiscal planning for 40–1; use of resource funds 39–40; World Bank report on Ghanaian government's utilisation of 11, 82; *see also* mineral royalties; rent-seeking theory; revisionist theory of natural resource management

mineral resources: abundance found in Ghana 2; belong to Ghanaian state 8; benefitting elites in Africa 4; issues around ownership/control/management of 6, 86–8, 103–4, 111–12; as percentage of total merchandise exports 3; wastes created by 93, 117; *see also* governance of mineral resources

Mineral Revenue Management Act 85, 107, 113

mineral revenues *see* mineral rents/revenues

mineral rights 5, 6, 8, 103

mineral royalties: and citizens' access to information on 89–90, 90, 104, 105; community development via responsible use of 84, 85,

88, 91; disbursement of, lack of transparency/accountability in 104, 107–8; disbursement of, players involved in 10–11; flat rate of 5% tax on profits 10; increases in mineral royalty revenue 3; percentage redistributed to local communities 2, 7; recommendations of Commission of Enquiry 6; *see also* mineral rents/revenues

Minerals Act (1962) 6, 6–7

Minerals and Mining Act (2006) 7, 8, 10, 10–11, 12, 14, 103, 106–7, 117

Minerals and Mining Amendment Act (2010) 10

Minerals and Mining Law (1986) 7

Minerals Commission of Ghana: funding of 107; interviews with officials from 50, 85–6, 89, 98, 103, 104, 106, 108; as player in mining sector 13, *13*; poor working relations with district assemblies 99

Minerals Development Fund (MDF) 2, 7, 10, *10*, 11, 83

Mining Act (2006) 7

mining companies: and citizens' perceptions of exploitation by 102; contribution to Ghanaian economy 2; and decision-making processes around selection of 88; and disclosure of information on taxes paid 90; introduction of 'alternative livelihood programme' 80, 102; large- and small-scale operations 7, 7–8, 14, 74, 81, 97, 109; major companies in Ghana 8, *9*; and options for utilisation of revenues for community development 91; and ownership/control of mineral resources 86, 87; and ownership of health facilities 76, 101; as player in mining sector *13*, 14; privatisation of 7, 12; profit-making vs community development 81–2, 82–3; role in prevention of pollution 116, 116–17; training of staff 3, 109; *see also* mineral rents/revenues; mineral royalties

mining contracts: and citizens' access
   to information on 8, 88–9, 104,
   105, 113; role of chiefs in 12
mining sector: and agricultural sector,
   impact on 79–80, 82, 93, 99, 101–2,
   103, 109–10, 115–16, 116; and
   citizens' access to information on
   8, 88–90, 104–5, 106–7, 112, 113;
   contribution to Ghana's economy
   3; and employment, as source of 2–
   3, 4, 20, 27, 61, 79–81, 83, 84, 101,
   102; and employment, equitable
   participation in 92–3, 94, 109, *112*;
   environmental impact of 80, 82,
   84, 93, 94, 101, 103, 109–10, 116–
   17; environmental regulations for
   116; government actions to attract
   investment in 7; illegal mining 74,
   80, 81, 93, 97, 102, 109, 112–13;
   institutional and legal framework
   7–12; mining as main occupation
   of respondents 79, 101; need for
   integration with other sectors 99,
   115; need for intergration with
   other sectors 94; and participation,
   need for inclusivity in 88, 91, 94,
   114–15, 117; players involved in 12,
   13–14; proposals for contributions
   to social development 83; and
   transparency/accountability,
   need for reinforcement of 8, 105,
   112, 117; *see also* regulation of
   mining sector
Moore, M. 36
Morris, M. 26
mortality rates 32, 74, 77–8
Moss, T. 23, 24
Muslim religion 58

National Health Insurance Scheme
   (NHIS) 74, 76, 76–7, 77, 101, 114
natural resource rents 20
natural resources: correlation with
   authoritarianism 23; correlation
   with civil wars 23; correlation
   with economic development 20,
   24, 24–5, 27; OECD definition of
   28; resource wealth as obstacle to
   democracy 22; revisionist theory
   of management of 25–41, 111;
   see also mineral resources

Nigeria 37, 40
non-governmental organisations
   (NGOs): citizens' knowledge/
   awareness of 90–1; critical
   of government's approach to
   marginalised groups 14; as player
   in mining sector 13, *13*; role as
   'watchdogs' 37; as source of
   access to information on mining
   revenues 89; as source of education
   funding 69; *see also* civil society
   organisations; Wassa Association
   of Communities Affected by
   Mining (WACAM)
non-renewable natural resources 28
Norway 26, 33, 35, 39
nuclear family system 54
Nukunya, G.K. 54, 56
nursery schools 68, 69
nurses 78

observations, as data collection
   instrument 46, 49, 50
occupations of household heads
   60–1, 61, 79, 101
oil sector: and Dutch disease 24;
   Minerals Commission official's
   views on benefits of 85; as non-
   renewable natural resource
   28; oil wealth as obstacle to
   democracy 22, 23, 32; receipts
   from oil exports 3; as source of
   African FDI 27; as source of
   revenue generation 37, 101; and
   use of transfer through pricing
   strategy 34
'Olson effect' 21
Open Society Institute (OSI) 37, 39
ordinance marriages 58
Organisation for Economic
   Co-operation and Development 28
Ossowski, R. 40
ownership: of health facilities 76,
   101; of mineral resources 6, 86,
   87–8, 103–4, 112
owners-occupiers of houses 63
Oxford Poverty and Human
   Development Initiative 4

Pacto Fiscal (Guatemala) 36
Parliament 14, 19–20, 89, 104, 112–13

participation: equitable participation
in mining employment 92–3, 94,
109, *112*; as important governance
concept 18, 30, 31; and need for
community involvement in mining
sector 88, 91, 94, 114–15, 117;
participatory process used in PRSP
36; as tool to tackle resource curse
35, 35–6
patrilineal families 54
PAYE contributions 3
pensioners 61
perching 63
physically challenged persons 92, 94,
109, 115
platinum 1
policies, mineral 5–7, 51
policymaking 14
political economy: often neglected
connection between politics and
economy 20; and revisionist theory
of natural resource management 26
political rents 20
pollution, mining 80, 82, 84, 93, 94,
101, 103, 109–10, 116–17
polyclinics 75, *75*
population: of Ghana 2; of Prestea
Huni Valley 47; of Sekondi-
Takoradi metropolitan area 47; of
Tarkwa Nsuaem 47, 68, 78
poverty: as characteristic of the
resource curse 32; correlation
with natural resources wealth
24–5; importance of education
in eradication of 67; poverty
reduction strategies 12, 20, 36,
36–7, 86, 117; and profits made by
mining companies 81–2; as result
of skewed development patterns
in mineral wealth countries
32; and revisionist theory of
natural resource management 27;
widespread in Ghana 4, 97–8;
World Bank definition of 62
power cuts 64
Precious Minerals Marketing
Company 13
Prestea Huni Valley 47, *48*, 49
primary (basic) education 59, 68, 69,
70, 99, 100
primary data 50–1

private educational institutions
72, 99–100
private health facilities 75, 76, 101
private sector 29, 30, 31, 33, 36, 38
privatisation 7, 12
procurement 115
professional sector 60, 61
profit-making vs community
development 81–2, 82–3
Provisional National Defence
Council (PNDC) 6–7, *7*
public educational institutions
69, 72, 99
Public Finance Monitoring Centre
(Azerbaijan) 37
public health: facilities in Western
Region 75, 76, 101; as measure of
socio-economic status 66; *see also*
healthcare
Publish What You Pay initiative 39
purposive sampling 47

qualitative data, as data collection
instrument 46, 49–51
quality: of education 72–4, 100; of
healthcare 77–9, 101, 114; of living
conditions 97–9
questionnaires, as data collection
instrument 49–50, 51

random sampling 47, 49
regulation of mining sector: calls
for additional regulatory body
91; and engagement in illegal
mining 74, 80, 81, 93, 97, 102, 109,
112–13; environmental damage
caused by unregulated mining
93; expenditure of MDF funds
on 11; framework provided by
Minerals and Mining Act 107, 117;
importance of compliance with 18;
lack of community participation
in 88; need for transparency/
accountability in 112; regulatory
institutions 12–14, 98
regulations on environment 116
religion of case study respondents 58
renewable natural resources 28
renting of houses 63
rents *see* mineral rents/revenues
rent-seeking theory 20–5, 111

'repression effect' of rents 22–3
research methodology of case
study 46–52
resource curse: Africa as paradox of
plenty or suffering 1; avoided by
some mineral wealth countries 33;
rent-seeking theory explanations
for 23; views of revisionist theorists
on 25–6, 26–7, 27, 32, 33, 35–6;
ways of beating 117
resource funds 39–40
resources *see* mineral resources;
natural resources
retail/sales sector 60, 61, 83
retrenchments 81
revenues *see* mineral rents/revenues;
mineral royalties
Revenue Watch Institute 8, 39
reviews of documents 49, 51
revisionist theory of natural resource
management 25–41, 111
rights to minerals 5, 6, 8, 103
Right to Information Bill 113
rooms, number of 63
Ross, M.L. 22
royalties *see* mineral royalties
Rozner, S. 35–6, 36, 37, 38, 39, 40,
41, 107

Sala-i-Martin, X. 24
sales/retail sector 60, 61, 83
sampling methods 47, 49
sanitation 66, 98
Schneider, A. 36
scholarships 68, 74, 113
schools 67–70, 71–2, 99–100
Schultz's Citizen's Guide 38–9
secondary education 59, 68, 69, 70,
99, 100
Sekondi-Takoradi metropolitan area
(STMA) 47, *48*, 49
Senior High School Certificate
Examination 73
services sector 60, 61
Siegle, J. 31–2, 32, 33
single heads of household 57
size of households 59–60
skilled labour 25, 80–1, 93, 109
skills development 67, 94, 99, 102
small-scale mining companies 7, 7–8,
14, 74, 81, 97, 109

Social and Economic Rights Action
Centre (Nigeria) 37
social development 1, 27, 28, 32, 40,
83; *see also* development
socio-economic development: mining
sector's potential for promotion
of 84–6, 91, 103, 108; people's
productive qualities critical for 99;
promoted via effective governance
of mineral resources 111, 114;
public health as measurement
of 66; and rent-seeking theory
21; transparency/accountability
in promotion of 102; *see also*
development
South Africa: distribution of natural
resources rents 34; major mining
companies in *9*; use of natural
resources for development 26, 33
'spending effect' of rents 22
standard of living: and age of
household heads 56; linked
to low-income earning 62; as
measurement of development
4, 65; and role of mining in
improvement of 99; and type of
house 63
Standing, A. 10, 11, 12, 88
state *see* Ghana; government of
Ghana; local government
state-owned enterprises 7
stool lands 6, 8–10, 10–11, *10*
stratified sampling 47, 49
street lights 64–5
structural dependency theory
81, 102–3
Subramanian, A. 24
sustainable development 27, 31, 67,
87–8, 117
Sweden 26, 27

Tarkwa Nsuaem municipality: data
on education 68, 69, 70, 72, 72–3,
73, 100; data on healthcare 75, 76,
78, 101; map of *48*; selected as case
study area 47, 49
taxation: citizens' access to
information on 89, 90, 104, 105;
mining sector as highest taxpayer
to GRA 3; reduction of income
tax to attract investment 7; and

rent-seeking theory 21, 22, 23, 24; role of fiscal pacts 36; royalty flat rate of 5% tax on profits 10; and strategies for spending natural resources rents 33–4; use of taxes to develop communities 91
teachers 72–3, 100, 113, 116
technical sector 60, 61
technical/vocational institutions 68, 70, 73, 99, 100, 113
tenure of dwellings 63
tertiary education 59, 68–9, 69, 70, 99, 100, 113
Tilton, J.E. 25, 27
toilet facilities 66, 98
trading sector 79, 80, 83, 84, 101, 102
traditional authorities: accused of lack of transparency/accountability in utilisation of revenues 12, 85, 88, 104; composition of 8–10, 104; critical role in governance of mining sector 12; disbursements of revenues to *10*, 11, 12, 104, 105, 107, 107–8; enable access to mining job opportunities 94, 109; engagement in illegal/unregulated mining 113; misappropriation of revenues 107–8; and ownership/control of mineral resources 6, 86, 87, 104; as player in mining sector 13, *13*
training: to enable alternative livelihood strategies 116; and importance of local content policy 115; limited number of educational institutions for 99; of mining company staff 3, 109; need for investment of mineral revenues in 113, 114
transfer through pricing strategy 34
transparency: overview/definitions of 17, 107; calls for promotion of via legislation 91, 94; Chamber of Mines official's views on 106; and citizens' access to information on mining contracts/payments 88–90, 106–7; Extractive Industries Transparency Initiative *13*, 38, 90, 105, 106, 107–8; Fiscal Transparency Code of Good Practices 38; in

government budget formulation/implementation 37; and importance of high literacy rates 59; lacking in chiefs' utilisation of revenues 12, 85, 88, 104; lacking in policy on MDF 11; linked to benefits from resource wealth 33; in Minerals and Mining Act 106–7; Minerals Commission official's views on 106; needed in distribution of natural resources rents 34; needs reinforcing in mining sector 8, 105, 112, 117; as part of human-centred resource governance approach 112, *112*; pivotal to good governance 31, 83, 102; promoted via Publish What You Pay initiative 39; promoted via stakeholder engagement in mining sector 114; Revenue Watch Institute, work of 39; as tool to tackle resource curse 35; WACAM official's views on 106–7; will be enhanced by Right to Information Bill 113; *see also* accountability
Transparency Index 8
Tsikata, F.S. 5, 6, 7

unemployment 60, 61, 62, 72, 80, 81, 102, 114; *see also* employment
United Kingdom: colonial mining policy 5; Department for International Development *13*, 35, 38; launch of EITI 38; launch of Publish What You Pay initiative 39; use of natural resources for development 26
United Nations, definition of a house 62
United Nations Development Programme (UNDP): affirmation of importance of education 66–7; definition of governance 29, 30; measurement of human development 4
United Nations Environment Programme (UNEP) 31
United States of America *9*, 26, 27
University of Ghana 67, 102
unskilled/manual labour 60, 81, 93, 94, 109, 115

Vincente, P.C. 23
vocational/technical institutions 68,
    70, 73, 99, 100, 113

Wassa Association of Communities
    Affected by Mining (WACAM):
    citizens' knowledge/awareness of
    91; interviews with officials from
    50, 90, 98, 105, 106–7, 107–8; as
    mining sector player *13*; survey
    on mining sector's benefits to
    communities 85
waste: management of 66, 98, 108,
    117; mineral wastes 93, 117
water: pollution of 94, 103, 109, 116;
    supply of 65, 88, 98
West African Senior School
    Certificate Examination 73
Western Region of Ghana: and
    educational issues in 67–74,
    99–100; electricity connection in
    64; employment opportunities in
    mining sector 79–81, 83, 92–3,
    94; issues around healthcare
    74–9, 100–1; living conditions in
    97–9; map of *48*; and ownership
    of mineral resources 86; rich
    in mineral resources 2; selected
    as case study area 47; *see also*
    Ghana; heads of households
women: and composition of
    case study households 60; and
    equal opportunities in mining
    employment 92, 109; as heads of
    households 55–6; and importance
    of local content policy 115; and
    need for alternative livelihood
    strategies 116
World Bank: definition of
    governance 28–9, 30; definition
    of poverty 62; as player in mining
    sector *13*; Poverty Reduction
    Strategy Process 36; report on use
    of mineral revenues to promote
    development 11, 82; study of the
    economies of mining countries 1
World Health Organization 78

Yanez-Pagans, M. 35
Young, L. 23, 24
youth: and engagement in mining
    activities 74, 80, 81; lacking in
    employment opportunities 102, 115;
    lacking in skills 81; and need for
    alternative livelihood strategies 116;
    widespread unemployment of 81

For Product Safety Concerns and Information please contact our EU
representative GPSR@taylorandfrancis.com
Taylor & Francis Verlag GmbH, Kaufingerstraße 24, 80331 München, Germany

www.ingramcontent.com/pod-product-compliance
Lightning Source LLC
Chambersburg PA
CBHW061749270326
41928CB00011B/2441

9 780367 507183